D1410115

AQUARIUM PLANTS

AQUARIUM PLANTS

NIELS JACOBSEN

Illustrations by
Verner Hancke

Translated and adapted by
Gwynne Vevers

BLANDFORD PRESS
POOLE   DORSET

First published in the English language 1979
Copyright © 1979 Blandford Press Ltd.
Link House, West Street
Poole, Dorset BH15 1LL

ISBN 0 7137 0865 4

Vevers, Gwynne
  Aquarium plants.
  1. Aquarium plants – Identification
  I. Title   II. Hancke, Verner
  III. Jacobsen, Niels. Akvarieplanter i farver.
  Adaptations
  635.9′674   SF457.7

Originally published in Danish as *Akvarieplanter i Farver*
World copyright © 1977 Politkens Forlag, Copenhagen

Phototypeset by Oliver Burridge & Co. Ltd, Crawley
Text printed in Great Britain by Fletcher & Sons Ltd., Norwich
Colour plates printed by The Ysel Press Ltd., Deventer, Netherlands
Books bound by Richard Clay (Chaucer Press) Ltd., Bungay, Suffolk

Contents

Acknowledgements

The publishers wish to thank the Botanical Museum and the Botanical Garden in Copenhagen who made their collections available and Holger Windelør of 'Tropica' in Aarhus, Denmark, who supplied a large part of the living material and gave much advice on cultivation.

Preface

This book, like its companion *Aquarium Fishes in Colour*,* is intended primarily as an identification guide for aquarists. It describes and illustrates about 200 aquatic plant species—a very representative selection of the species that can be bought for and grown in the home aquarium.

The plants illustrated in the colour plates have been drawn from living specimens and, with a few exceptions, to the same scale (half natural size). In most cases they show the flowers, although these do not usually appear in the aquarium. Aquatic plants can normally be identified without flowers, but a flowering specimen will make the identification even more reliable.

The book starts with a brief introduction on aquarium plants in general. This is followed by the colour plates and the descriptions of the plants. The plants are arranged in systematic order in both the plates and the descriptive text. In addition to the species depicted in the plates, the text also includes other closely related species. In the case of the larger genera, there is a brief introduction before the individual species are described. The species descriptions are supplemented by line drawings, most of which show characters of systematic importance.

The species descriptions include the scientific name, any synonyms, any English names, distribution, characteristics, habitat, aquarium conditions, temperature and general remarks. Synonyms indicated by inverted commas are not to be regarded as true botanical synonyms, but rather as erroneous names that have appeared in various aquarium publications.

The experienced aquarist will possibly notice that certain species are not included. The selection has been made on the basis of those plants that are available on the market, bearing in mind that these are mostly plants that come from the tropics.

* Blandford Press, Poole, 1975.

The Bibliography on page 156 includes general botanical handbooks and a few scientific articles of special interest.

There is a brief glossary of botanical terms located immediately before the plant descriptions and an index of the scientific names of the plants described, plus an index of the few English names that are in common usage.

Aquarium Plants in General

During the last 10-20 years, the choice of aquarium fishes and plants has changed considerably, and it is now true to say that the field is dominated by species from the tropics. Those plants which are not suitable for heated tanks are gradually disappearing.

Aquarists want their tanks to look natural, and in most cases this means that they will try to give them the appearance of an underwater scene in a tropical rain-forest stream. To some, an aquarium tank with fishes and plants is like a garden, and this is probably the most satisfactory way of looking at it.

Aquatic plants should be grown in the same way as other plants. They require water, light, nutrients and soil. They should be planted at a certain depth, weeded and transplanted, and can often be propagated by cuttings. Some have to be severely pruned to prevent them growing too luxuriantly, others have to be protected from disturbance. Aquarium plants come from widely differing habitats and require widely differing living conditions. Just as fishes require the correct conditions if they are to thrive, so also do plants.

This introductory section is intended to give general advice on the planting and cultivation of aquarium plants.

Where the plants come from

A knowledge of the conditions under which plants grow in the wild is an essential prerequisite to keeping them in the aquarium.

An important factor in assessing the character of a soil or a water is its degree of acidity or alkalinity. This can be defined numerically by its hydrogen ion concentration, usually expressed as its pH. If the pH is below 7 the soil or water is acid, but if it is above 7 it is alkaline (basic); a pH of 7 is neutral. The pH can be measured with indicator paper, indicator solutions or a pH meter. A general understanding of the effect of pH on the growth of plants is quite important.

The various nutrient substances found in soil and in water influence one another in different ways depending upon the conditions. For example, the addition of calcium results in an increase in the pH. At a high pH plants have difficulty in taking up iron, which is more accessible to them at lower pH values. Iron is essential for the metabolism of plants and excess calcium can thus cause iron deficiency, resulting in poor growth or the death of the plants. Similarly, manganese is least accessible at pH 6·5-7·5, and copper at pH 5·5-6·5.

Investigations on the uptake of phosphorus by plants have shown that this is inhibited when the pH is in the range 5·5-8·0. Similarly, an increase in the amount of nitrate may inhibit the uptake of phosphorus, and conversely an increase in phosphorus can inhibit the uptake of nitrogen.

As a score or so of other substances may be involved in plant metabolism, the problems become very involved.

Aquarium water often contains nitrate, and has a high pH. It is, in fact, preferable to keep the pH at 6·0-6·5.

A considerable amount is known about the reactions of land plants to soil conditions, but this knowledge is not necessarily applicable to conditions in water. In fact, not much is known about the requirements of underwater plants and in the aquarium it is often necessary to experiment.

There are two principal types of freshwater habitat, namely running waters and standing waters. This is a fairly rough generalization, but it is sufficient for ordinary purposes.

At certain times of the year plants growing in standing waters suffer from a deficiency of certain substances, and this limits their growth. In such conditions, plants may stop growing, become reduced in numbers or enter a resting phase until the substances concerned are again present in sufficient amounts. Plants require several different substances for normal growth, but if only one of these is absent their growth may cease.

Plants growing in rivers usually receive a steady supply of

utrient salts throughout the year. This supply may be relatively
nall, but is usually sufficient.

During recent years, investigations have been carried out on
ome of the rivers in southern Thailand, which form the habitat
f *Crinum thaianum*, *Barclaya longifolia* and *Cryptocoryne siamensis*.
everal surprising results were obtained, but the most remarkable
iscovery was the presence of very large amounts of iron in solu-
on. In the aquarium, on the other hand, dissolved iron only
ccurs in small amounts and is one of the factors limiting plant
rowth. It was also shown that the rivers had a low content of
itrate whereas this substance often occurs in large amounts in
quarium tanks. Most aquarium plants have come originally from
unning waters so their transplantation into an aquarium involves
complete upset of their living conditions, and some of the sub-
tances they require may be completely lacking.

etting up the aquarium

n speaking of an aquarium we mean an ordinary community
ank.

An aquarium tank must be sufficiently large, and some would
ay the larger the better. In fact, aquatic plants will not thrive in a
olume of water less than 60 litres (13 imp. or 16 U.S. gallons).
n practice, it is better to set the minimum volume at 100 litres
22 imp. or 26 U.S. gallons). With a large volume of water it is
asier to establish and maintain a good balance and keep the plants
nd fishes in good condition.

UBSTRATE

)pinions differ on what constitutes the ideal substrate for an
quarium tank. This is partly because there are several miscon-
eptions regarding the uptake of nutrients by plants. With a few
xceptions plants have roots, and these serve for anchorage and
or the uptake of nutrients. In general, this also applies to aquatic
lants.

Many aquarium plants are, in fact, marsh plants which unde certain conditions can grow underwater. Their root system is ofte very well developed and adapted for taking up nutrients. It is onl the purely aquatic plants, such as *Vallisneria*, *Elodea* and *Cabombo* which take up a large proportion of their nutrients through thei leaves. In fact, there are several transitional stages from terrestria plants to purely aquatic plants and it would therefore be wrong t make sweeping generalizations on the methods by which plant acquire their nutrients.

At the present time it has become customary for the substrate t consist of sand which has been thoroughly washed before use. Wit this method the last traces of plant nutrient have been remove from the tank. The theory is that the lack of nutrients will b balanced by manuring due to the excreta of the fish populatio This may take place, but it will take some 6 months for this suppl of manure to become effective and in the meantime the plants wi suffer from starvation.

The substrate should have a lower layer of fine gravel (diamete 1-3 mm) mixed with clay, weathered granite or other similar sub stance, but without any significant content of organic matte Above this there should be a layer of slightly coarser grav (diameter 2-4 mm) without any admixture. The whole substrat should be quite deep (8-10 cm) so that the roots of the plants hav something to penetrate. It does not matter if the substrate rise above the level of the tank frame.

If the weathered granite or other mineral has not been inco porated from the start, it is possible to add it at a later stage. Thi can be done, for instance, by injecting it into the substrate, usin a wide-bore plastic injection syringe.

The use of garden soil in an aquarium tank is not recommende It has a high content of plant remains that have not rotted dow and these will soon start to decompose. In the wild this happe quite naturally, but in the aquarium it cannot be controlled.

LIGHTING

Nowadays fluorescent tubes are used almost universally for lightin

quarium tanks. They are inexpensive to run and give a good out-
put of light. Tungsten lamps are only used on certain occasions,
nd usually to supplement fluorescent tubes.

There are several different types of fluorescent tubes on the
market. These are either given names, such as 'daylight' and 'warm
white' or numbers. The tubes made by Philips Electrical Ltd. are
given numbers, as shown below. The nearest equivalent colours for
he tubes made by other manufacturers are given in brackets.
There are also special growth-promoting tubes used in the horti-
ultural industry, such as Fluora (Osman) and Gro-lux (Sylvania),
both of which are coded as 'gro' in the following notes.

Thus, when only one fluorescent tube is to be used above a tank,
olour 32 (de luxe warm white or warmtone) or 33 (daylight)
vould be the best. Using two tubes there can be other combina-
ions, such as

$$gro + 32 \text{ or } 33$$

or with 3 tubes

$$gro + 33 + 33$$

and so on.

There are innumerable combinations, the main object being to
obtain as much as possible of the natural spectrum and, parti-
ularly, to ensure that there is sufficient red light. When used alone
he special growth-promoting tubes have no advantage over the
others but they are beneficial when used in combination with the
other types.

The characteristics of some of the suitable tubes are given below:

colour 32   moderate but adequate blue; high red content
colour 33   moderate content of blue and red
Gro-lux/Fluora   high content of blue and red.

For a detailed comparison of the spectrum emitted by the
different types of tube it would be necessary to study the spectral
curves.

Dutch ornamental aquaria are among the best that can be

found. As an example, some of the aquarium tanks which gained
the highest awards in 1972 had the lighting systems shown in the
following table.

A selection of lighting systems for tanks containing different
volumes of water.

Tank volume (litres)	Power requirement (watts) for type of lamp			
	32	33	gro	tungsten
350	150	65	20	
370	70	45	25	40
500	180			80
550	160		80	
625	80		80	

When changing fluorescent tubes it is good practice to lay a
strip of newspaper (10-15 cm broad) below the light until the
plants have become accustomed to the new light intensity. The
amount of light can be gradually increased by cutting strips of
the paper.

As a general rule an aquarium tank should be lit for about 15
hours a day.

HEATING

Most tropical aquarium tanks should be kept at a temperature of
$24-26°C \pm 2°$. This temperature is not always the most suitable for
the plants, but in practice most will live in it.

The temperature will often be 2-4°C lower in the substrate than
it is in the water. This tends to inhibit plant growth. One method

raising the substrate temperature is to have a false bottom through which the warm aquarium water can be circulated, either by a water circulation pump or by an air pump.

The water in the substrate can also be warmed by passing it through a substrate filter.

WATER

In many cases aquarists have to use mains water, without regard to its quality. In fact, most plants can become accustomed to mains water, even though its content of minerals varies considerably from place to place.

FILTRATION

A system of filtration is not actually necessary for the plants in an aquarium, but it does equalize the temperature by moving the water around, and this is an advantage to the plants.

There are several types of substrate filter and most are very efficient. From the viewpoint of the plants, the principle is that they are firmly anchored while water containing nutrients circulates past the roots which then grow rapidly. If substrate filtration is to be beneficial to the plants, the water must contain a certain amount of nutrient. Care should be taken that certain minerals, such as iron, are not deficient, but good results can be obtained by using the special fertilizers prepared for aquarium use (see under fertilizers).

Photosynthesis

Light is a form of energy, and plants which contain the green pigment chlorophyll can harness and use this energy, together with water and nutrients, to build up substances such as carbohydrates, starch and cellulose. This process, which is known as photosynthesis, involves the production of oxygen. If green plants receive insufficient light their living processes will stop and they will finally die.

Some water plants, particularly the purely aquatic ones, take u
carbon in the form of bicarbonate, whereas those which can b
broadly categorized as submerged marsh plants mainly acquir
carbon in the form of carbon dioxide. Bicarbonate uptake occu
principally in those plants which grow in water with a high pH.

Nutrients

As in land plants, many aquatic plants take up mineral salts o
nutrients through the roots, but some take up these substance
through their leaves.

Apart from oxygen, hydrogen and carbon, plant nutrients ca
be divided into various groups, namely:

a) elements which are used in large amounts, e.g. nitrogen, pho:
   phorus, potassium, calcium, sulphur, magnesium and iron;
b) elements, known as trace elements, which are used in very sma
   amounts, e.g. manganese, zinc, boron, copper and molyl
   denum;
c) elements which have been shown to be important for th
   normal growth of certain plants, e.g. sodium, aluminiun
   silicon, chlorine, gallium and cobalt.

In the absence of some of these elements, plants may suffer fro
deficiency diseases. The symptoms of deficiencies are often difficu
to define accurately as there are several factors involved. In part
cular, different plant species react in different ways to deficiencie
of the various elements. The most common symptoms are liste
below.

Nitrogen deficiency   the leaves turn yellow, the older ones doing s
first. The plants may also become reddish from the presence of th
red pigment anthocyanin.

Phosphorus deficiency   similar to nitrogen deficiency. Prematur
leaf-fall and anthocyanin formation. The leaves may also sho
dead areas, and the plants appear sickly.

Calcium deficiency   growing points on the stem, leaves and root ti
show signs of damage and may die off. The edges of young leav
often become yellow.

Magnesium deficiency   the leaves show yellow spots, at first on th older ones, later on the younger ones. There may be anthocyanin formation.

Potassium deficiency   yellow areas on the leaves, followed by withering of the leaf edges and tips. These symptoms appear first in the older parts of the plant.

Sulphur deficiency   similar to nitrogen deficiency, but appearing first in the young leaves.

Iron deficiency   the leaves turn yellow, the young ones first. They often have a reticulate appearance with the greenish nerves enclosing yellow leaf tissue. If the plants are not given a supplement of iron, each new leaf becomes increasingly yellow and the plant finally dies. Fast-growing aquarium plants, e.g. *Echinodorus* and *Hygrophila*, are the first to show iron deficiency.

Manganese deficiency   areas of dead, yellowish tissue between the leaf nerves.

Copper deficiency   the tips of the leaves die and the edges wither.

Zinc deficiency   in older leaves yellowish areas appear between the nerves, starting at the leaf tip and along the edges.

Boron deficiency   the shoot tips die and the plant produces side shoots whose tips also die quite soon.

Molybdenum deficiency   yellow spots appear between the leaf nerves on the older leaves, followed by brownish areas along the edges. Flowering is inhibited.

Anthocyanin formation is not often seen in aquarium plants as this process requires a large amount of light.

Fertilizers

Aquarium substrates can be enriched by the addition of 'manure', often in the form of one of the aquarium fertilizers available on the market. Alternatively, a general fertilizer of the type used, for example, for house plants, can also be employed. When using an aquarium fertilizer the instructions should be followed most carefully.

House plant fertilizers must be used very carefully, as these are poisonous even in very low concentrations. They contain, for example, nitrates which are highly undesirable substances for fishes, as they can very quickly form particularly dangerous compounds. A dose of 5% of the normal house plant concentration is sufficient, and under certain conditions even such a small amount as this may prove poisonous to the fishes. On the whole, it is really better to use the rather more expensive special aquarium fertilizers rather than to buy new, even more expensive fishes.

Depending upon the plants and the amount of light it may be very difficult to determine whether there is sufficient fertilizer in the water, or whether the plants are using up some substances faster than others. There is a serious risk of overdosing. It is often a good idea to change a proportion of the water each time fertilizer is added. In general it is better to add very small amounts of fertilizer at frequent intervals, but even this will only be necessary in tanks with rapidly growing plants. In newly planted tanks it is advisable to use little or no fertilizer until the plants have had a chance to become established.

One of the substances which it is sometimes advantageous to add is iron. The simplest method of doing this is to add the substance known as Fe-EDTA (ethylenediaminetetra-acetic acid-Fe-Na-chelator). In water, this substance releases iron in a form which the plants can absorb. A stock solution is made up by dissolving 2·8 grams of Fe-EDTA in 1 litre of water. The dose added should be 1 millilitre of the stock solution to every litre of tank water.

Propagation

In the aquarium it is generally true to say that propagation of the plants by seeds is only of importance in a few genera such as *Aponogeton*, *Ottelia* and *Blyxa*. The fact that most aquarium plants are grown submerged inhibits flowering and therefore the chance of seeds being set. On the other hand, most aquarium plants can be propagated very easily by vegetative means, i.e. runners or cuttings, or in some cases from plants arising at the leaf edges.

Mature plants can often be put directly into the aquarium tank, but it is sometimes better to raise cuttings in a separate tank and to plant them out in the aquarium when they are well rooted, which may take a matter of 2–5 months.

Methods of propagation are discussed under the various plant species, but there is one general point to be mentioned here. Plants that grow up to the water surface, e.g. *Hygrophila, Ludwigia, Rotala, Hydrilla, Limnophila*, should be cut back frequently, thus producing cuttings which can be planted out. Depending upon the conditions it may be necessary to prune such plants about once a month. When striking the cuttings it should be remembered that at least one node should be buried in the substrate.

How to plant

The positioning of the plants in an aquarium tank will naturally depend upon the species.

The tank is best planted before it is filled with water. The plants should each be placed in a hole in the substrate in such a way that the roots are covered, except in the case of *Vallisneria*.

A tank can also be planted after it has been filled with water, but this is not so convenient as the plants already in position tend to wave about in the water and get in the way of later plantings.

In general, the plants of each species should be planted in groups, and depending upon the species they should be separated from each other by a distance of 2-4 cm.

The plants should be inspected at least every week, for some will require to have dead leaves removed and those that grow fast will need to be pruned. At times, too, it may be necessary to change the position of some plants so that they can be seen to greater effect.

The choice of plants depends upon the purpose of the aquarium. In many cases plants are only used for aesthetic reasons. Most tanks have only a limited amount of space for plants, and it must be remembered that if these are properly kept they will grow.

As already mentioned the requirements of aquarium plants vary considerably. For example, it is difficult to grow *Egeria* and *Cryptocoryne* together in the same tank as they need quite different types of water. Fast-growing species have a tendency to smother those that grow slowly. Shade-loving plants can be grown in the shade of those that require plenty of light.

It is advisable to place the larger plants at the back of the tank,

the smaller ones in front. The scale of planting can vary, alway
remembering that there must be sufficient open water for the fishe
to swim in. It is a mistake to have too many different species as thi
would give a restless effect.

Algae

The following four groups of algae may be encountered in th
aquarium.

DIATOMS

These are microscopic plants which occur in enormous numbers
They often appear in newly established tanks where they form a
brownish film on leaves, rocks and glass. In most cases, howevei
diatoms do not persist in aquarium tanks.

GREEN ALGAE

Planktonic algae These are free-floating organisms consisting c
one or more cells. They occur when the water is particularly rich i
nutrients, possibly due to excess fish food, and when there is to
much light. It is then advisable to change a good proportion of th
water, decrease the amount of light and give less food.

Filamentous algae These occur as multicellular green filaments
often several centimetres long. They are a considerable nuisanc
and are not easy to get rid of. They are introduced to the tank eithe
with live food or with newly purchased plants. Not only are the
unattractive but they also inhibit the growth of the aquariun
plants by blocking the light and competing for nutrients. They ca
be treated with one of the compounds available on the market, o
a more drastic but efficient method is to clean out the tank ver
thoroughly and start again with new plants, taking care not t
re-introduce these troublesome algae.

Green film on rocks, plants and the aquarium glass. This is no
usually a serious problem and in most cases it can be controlled b
reducing the light and using less fertilizer.

BLUE-GREEN ALGAE

These are mostly unicellular organisms which thrive in polluted water. If they are a problem, it may be necessary to change the tank water, and if this is unsuccessful to change the substrate and give less food. The latter course may entail a reduction in the number of fishes.

RED ALGAE

These are primarily marine plants and there are only two forms which are of any importance in the freshwater aquarium. One is *Batrachospermum*, a slimy, branched, blue-green plant, 5-15 cm long, and somewhat similar to the filamentous algae mentioned above. It is not common in aquaria. The other is *Compsopogon*, the so-called pencil alga, which forms tufts, 0·5-1·5 cm high, on the leaves of aquatic plants. It may occur in large amounts and is difficult to eradicate. It can often be controlled by lowering the pH, but in general it is best dealt with by keeping the aquarium plants growing well so that they outstrip the algae.

Snails

These become a nuisance when they are present in large numbers and attack the plants. The Malayan pond snail (*Melanoides tuberculata*) burrows in the substrate, so that fish faeces are buried, and the top layer of the substrate becomes porous.

Chromosome numbers

The chromosomes are the carriers of the hereditary material in plants and animals. In plants they can be studied in the cells of the root tips and of the flower buds.

The number of chromosomes in a sexual cell (pollen grain or ovule) is designated as the haploid number n. When an ovule is pollinated the resulting fertilized egg will therefore have $2n$ chromosomes, and this is the diploid number. The basic number of chromosomes (n) may occur in multiples and form a polyploid series. Thus, $2n$ is diploid, $3n$ is triploid, $4n$ tetraploid, and so on.

Within the plant kingdom the chromosome numbers vary from $n=2$ to $n=$ about 500, but it is mostly in the range $n=5$ to 30. The size of the chromosomes varies from 0·0005 mm (e.g. in *Eleocharis*) to 0·025 mm (e.g. in *Crinum*). The chromosome picture of a plant, known as its karyotype, can be defined in terms of the number and size of the individual chromosomes and other attributes. The chromosome numbers are of importance in evaluating species complexes (as, for example, in the genus *Cryptocoryne*), but they are often of greater importance at the family and generic level.

The chromosome number is normally constant within a species, but there are instances in which, for example, diploid and tetraploid plants can scarcely be distinguished from one another, but where it would not be practical to regard them as two different species. The hybridization of a diploid and a tetraploid plant will produce sterile offspring. Doubling of the number of chromosomes occurs very commonly among plants.

The formation of polyploid series is one of the ways in which new forms may arise. Within a genus there may be plants in which, for example, $2n=12$, but there may also be plants with 24, 36 or 48 and so on, the basic number in this case being 6.

There may sometimes be morphological differences between, for example, diploid and tetraploid plants, which can therefore be separated systematically. In other cases, however, there may be no reliable characteristics on which to distinguish between such plants.

Plant names and the rules of botanical nomenclature

The scientific names of plants consist of two parts: a generic name, written with an initial capital letter, and a specific or species name starting with a lower case letter. These are Latin or latinized words. A name is only valid if the description of the plant is in accordance with the International Code for Botanical Nomenclature. This Code is intended to ensure the international standardization of plant names.

Linnaeus's book *Species Plantarum* published in 1753 is taken as he starting point. This means that the only valid names are those published after 1 May 1753. There are other starting points for the non-flowering plants.

One of the most important clauses in the Code concerns the principle of priority. The oldest valid published specific name must be used, even if the plant has subsequently been transferred to a different genus.

In order to be valid a new name must be accompanied by a description (after 1935 in Latin) published in a book or in a scientific journal.

When two different plants have been given the same name, e.g. *Cryptocoryne willisii* Reitz 1908 and *Cryptocoryne willisii* Engl. ex Baum 1909, the latter is invalid. The latter plant must have another name which in this case is *Cryptocoryne undulata* Wendt.

The basic systematic unit is the species. Several species are classified together in a genus (plural: genera), then genera are grouped into families, families into orders, and so on. A species may be subdivided into subspecies, varieties and forms.

When the name of a plant is cited, it is often customary to write the name of the person who gave the original description, e.g. *Egeria densa* Planchon. If the species is transferred to another genus, the original author's name is placed in parenthesis, while the name of the author who transferred the species is written at the end, e.g. *Elodea densa* (Planchon) Caspary.

Systematics

Many different plant groups have aquatic representatives. This book is concerned only with higher plants, i.e. those with a stem and leaves. Bacteria, fungi and algae are therefore not included.

The plant kingdom is divided into various higher groups or categories. The present section gives a brief account of the higher categories, while the families will be discussed together with the descriptions of the species. The names of the different groups have different endings depending upon the rank. Family names end in -aceae, e.g. Aponogetonaceae.

BRYOPHYTA (LIVERWORTS AND MOSSES)

These plants reproduce by means of spores which germinate and form the liverwort or moss plant which is haploid. This plant produces male and female organs. The male organs contain spermatozoids which swim off and fertilize female sex cells. This process $(n+n)$ results in the development of a sporophyte $(2n)$ which in turn produces spores (n).

In the Hepaticopsida (liverworts) the plant may be differentiated into stem and leaves, or it may be in the form of a broad branched thallus (Nos. 1-2).

In the Bryopsida, or mosses, the plant has a stem and leaves (Nos. 3-4).

PTERIDOPHYTA

Here there are three groups: the Lycopsida and Sphenopsida which are not represented in this book, and the Pteropsida or ferns, a group containing some aquatic forms.

Ferns reproduce by means of spores which are haploid. These germinate and grow into small scale-like plants which are often not more than 1 cm across. This is the prothallus, which develops male (antheridia) and female (archegonia) organs on its under side. The antheridia produce tiny motile spermatozoids while the archegonia produce egg-cells. Provided water is present the spermatozoids swim to the archegonia and fertilize the egg-cells which thus become diploid $(2n)$. The fertilized egg-cells grow into fern plants and these develop sori (singular: sorus) on their under side in which further spores are formed. The spores may be all of one type (isospores) or they may differ in size (heterospores), being either female macrospores or male microspores. The leaves or fronds are characterized by the fact that growth takes place at the tips (Nos. 5-13).

SPERMATOPHYTA (SEED OR FLOWERING PLANTS)

In this large group, reproduction involves the transfer of pollen to the ovules which are carried in the flowers. The Spermatophyta are subdivided into the Gymnospermae (conifers, etc.) which are not represented in this book, and the Angiospermae. In the latter the ovules are contained in carpels which are surrounded by stamens which in turn are enclosed in the perianth (petals and sepals), the whole forming the flower.

The Angiospermae have two groups, the Dicotyledones (dicotyledons) and the Monocotyledones (monocotyledons). In the former the embryo has two opposite seed leaves or cotyledons, and the seedling root usually persists and develops into a main root. The flowers usually have their parts arranged in multiples of 5 (pentamerous) or of 4 (tetramerous). This group contains the majority of the flowering plants (Nos. 14-53).

In the monocotyledons, the embryo plant has a single cotyledon. The seedling root soon ceases to grow and numerous side roots are formed. The flowers nearly always have parts arranged in threes (trimerous). The leaves often have parallel nerves. Many aquatic plants belong in this group (Nos. 54-134).

The Species concept

For a long time the species has been regarded as the natural unit in classifying living organisms, whether plants or animals. It is not always easy to define the exact scope of a given species, mainly because of the endless amount of variation shown by living organisms.

Since the publication in 1859 of Charles Darwin's *Origin of Species*, it has been generally accepted that the formation of species is a phenomenon which is continuous. Most studies on species formation, or speciation, have been concerned with diploid organisms showing cross-fertilization. Quite a few plants have neither cross-fertilizing diploids nor normal sexual reproduction. They may have self-fertilization, vegetative reproduction, seed formation without fertilization or various forms of chromosome variation.

The criteria on which to base the concept of a species will therefore vary from case to case. The species must be regarded as an approximation whose practical usefulness is obvious.

Individual plants occur in populations and the study of variation in individuals and populations and of their reproductive systems has led to what is known as the 'biological species concept'. The biological species may be very difficult to define in practical terms because so many factors are involved. There may, for example, be plants in which the evolution of the reproductive system does not always run parallel with external or morphological differences. It may, for instance, be very difficult to distinguish diploids from tetraploids, although they can be regarded as good biological species.

The separation of species is now based on as many criteria as possible. These include morphology, distribution, ecology, reproductive biology, and differences in chromosome numbers.

Even though two plants under experimental conditions can be hybridized and produce fertile offspring it does not necessarily follow that they should be regarded as the same species. There may, for example, be morphological differences, or the hybrids may not be able to establish themselves in the wild.

In most cases plants are still distinguished on purely morphological grounds. However, when there is continuous variation, e.g. over a large area of distribution, it may be necessary to enlarge the scope of a species and possibly to establish subspecies (ssp.) or varieties (var.).

The term subspecies is often used for ecological or geographical races which are sometimes connected by intermediate forms. Varieties have a lower status and differences between them are correspondingly less.

Glossary

BISEXUAL	flowers having both stamens and pistils
CORDATE	heart-shaped
COROLLA	petals
DIPLOID	a plant with twice the basic number of chromosomes
HAPLOID	the basic number of chromosomes, n
HASTATE	spear-shaped
HETEROSPOROUS	ferns having two different types of spore, namely macrospores and microspores
INFLORESCENCE	the flowering part of plants
ISOSPOROUS	ferns with spores all of the same size
MACROSPORES	see HETEROSPOROUS
MICROSPORES	see HETEROSPOROUS
NECTARY	small nectar-secreting body within a flower
PELTATE	a leaf attached by its lower surface rather than by its edge
PENTAMEROUS	flowers having the parts arranged in fives
PERIANTH	sepals and petals
PINNATE	a leaf with leaflets arranged on either side of a stalk
PINNATISECT	a pinnate leaf deeply cut into segments down to the midrib
POLYPLOID	a plant with several times the basic number of chromosomes
SAGITTATE	arrow-shaped
SORUS	in ferns, a group of spore-bearing structures
SPADIX	a fleshy axis with numerous sessile flowers
SPATHE	the bract surrounding an inflorescence in some plants
TETRAMEROUS	plants having the parts arranged in fours

TETRAPLOID   a plant with four times the basic number of
              chromosomes
THALLUS   plants not differentiated into stem and leaves
              (plural: thalli)
TRIMEROUS   flowers having the parts arranged in threes
TRIPLOID   a plant with three times the basic number of
              chromosomes
UNISEXUAL   flowers having either stamens or pistils

Measurements

For reasons of uniformity of presentation, metric units have been
used for all dimensions, capacities, etc. and the Celcius (Centi-
grade) scale for temperatures. Relevant conversion details are set
out below:

1 litre = 0·22 Imp. gallons
        = 0·264 U.S. gallons
1 gramme = 0·035 ounces
1 mm = 0·039 inches
1 cm = 0·394 inches

1 inch = 2·54 cm
       = 25·4 mm
1 Imp. gallon = 4·546 litres
1 U.S. gallon = 3·785 litres

Colour Plates

NOTE: The Latin names are incorrectly spelt on the captions to the following colour plates: 13, 15, 43, 68. The names are correct in the descriptions of the species.

1. Riccia fluitans
2. Ricciocarpus natans
3. Vesicularia dubyana
4. Leptodictyum riparium

5. Ceratopteris thalictroides
6. Bolbitis heudelotii

6

7. **Bolbitis heteroclita**
8. **Microsorium pteropus**
9. **Pilularia globulifera**

8

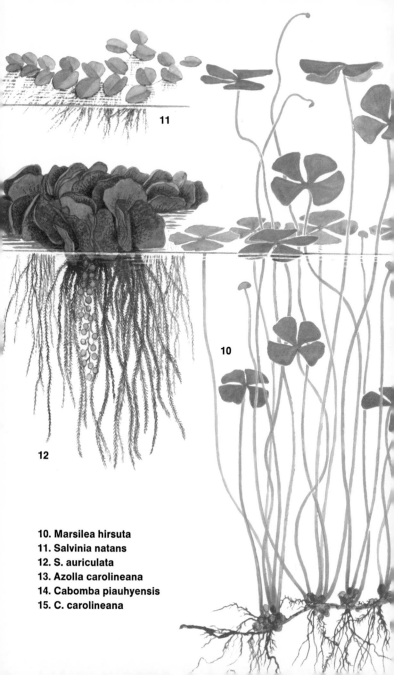

10. Marsilea hirsuta
11. Salvinia natans
12. S. auriculata
13. Azolla carolineana
14. Cabomba piauhyensis
15. C. carolineana

16. **Nuphar japonicum**
17. **N. lutea**
18. **Nymphaea pubescens**

16

17

18

19

19. **Nymphaea zenkeri**
20. **Barclaya longifolia**

21

23

21. Ceratophyllum demersum
22. Saururus cernuus
23. Alternanthera reineckii
24. Cardamine lyrata

22

22

24

25. Elatine macropoda
26. Samolus parviflorus
27. Hottonia palustris
28. Phyllanthus fluitans
29. Crassula helmsii
30. Aldrovanda vesiculosa
31. Didiplis diandra

27

29

25

32

33

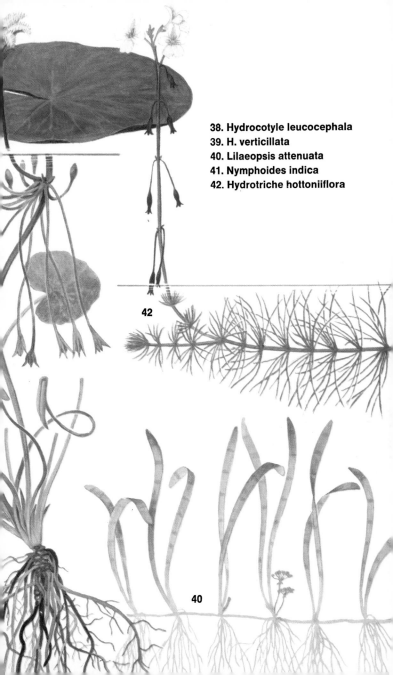

38. **Hydrocotyle leucocephala**
39. **H. verticillata**
40. **Lilaeopsis attenuata**
41. **Nymphoides indica**
42. **Hydrotriche hottoniiflora**

42

40

43   44   45

43. Bacopa carolineana
44. B. monnieri
45. Lindernia rotundifolia
46. Limnophila aquatica
47. L. sessiliflora
48. Micranthemum umbrosum
49. Utricularia gibba

50. **Hygrophila polysperma**
51. **H. difformis**
52. **H. guyanensis**
53. **H. corymbosa**

50

51

52   53

54. Vallisneria gigantea
55. V. natans v. natans
56. V. natans v. biwaensis
57. Blyxa aubertii

63

58

59

60

61

58. **Egeria densa**
59. **Lagarosiphon muscoides**
60. **Hydrilla verticillata**
61. **Elodea canadensis**
62. **Limnobium spongia**
63. **L. laevigatum**
64. **Ottelia alismoides**

65

65. Ottelia ulvifolia
66. Hydrocleis nymphoides
67. Echinodorus tenellus
68. E. magdalensis

69. Echinodorus maior
70. E. berteroi
71. E. bleheri

70

71

72

72a

72. Echinodorus osiris
73. E. macrophyllus

73

74

75

74. **Echinodorus horemanii**
75. **E. horizontalis**
76. **E. palaefolius v. latifolius**
77. **E. subalatus**
78. **E. cordifolius**

77

78

79

80

81

82

79. Sagittaria subulata
80. S. graminea v. graminea
81. S. graminea v. platyphylla
82. Aponogeton rigidifolius

83

84

83 Aponogeton crispus
chinatus
s

85

86

87

88

86. **Aponogeton ulvaceus**
87. **A. undulatus**
88. **A. boivinianus**

90

89

89. Aponogeton madagascariensis
90. Najas guadalupensis
91. Eriocaulon sexangulare
92. Xyris pauciflora

91

92

93. **Crinum thaianum**
94. **C. natans**

94

95. Eichhornia crassipes
96. Heteranthera zosterifolia
97. Zosterella dubia
98. Acorus gramineus v. gramineus
99. A. gramineus v. gramineus f. variegatis
100. A. gramineus v. pusillus

96   98   97   99

101. **Anubias nana**
102. **Spathiphyllum wallisii**
103. **Lagenandra ovata**

101

102   103

104. **Cryptocoryne ciliata**
105. **C. spiralis**
106. **C. parva**
107. **C. willisii**

108. Cryptocoryne beckettii
109. C. wendtii
110. C. undulata
111. C. lutea

109a

109b

109c

108

109

109d

110

111

112

112. **Cryptocoryne pontederiifolia**
113. **C. sarawacensis**
114. **C. johorensis**
115. **C. schulzei**

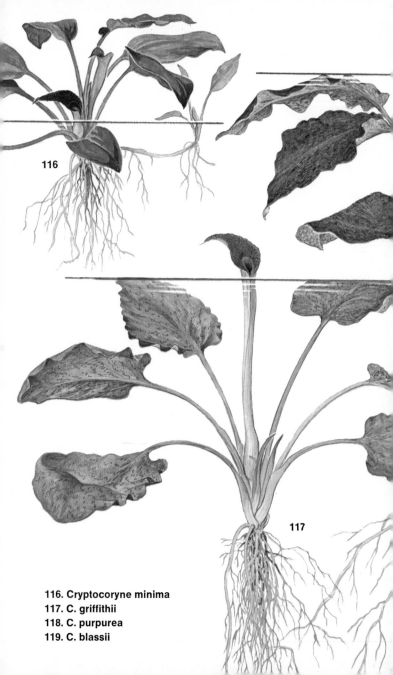

116. Cryptocoryne minima
117. C. griffithii
118. C. purpurea
119. C. blassii

118   119

120. **Cryptocoryne usteriana**
121. C. affinis
122. C. versteegii
123. C. lingua

123

121

124

126

127

128

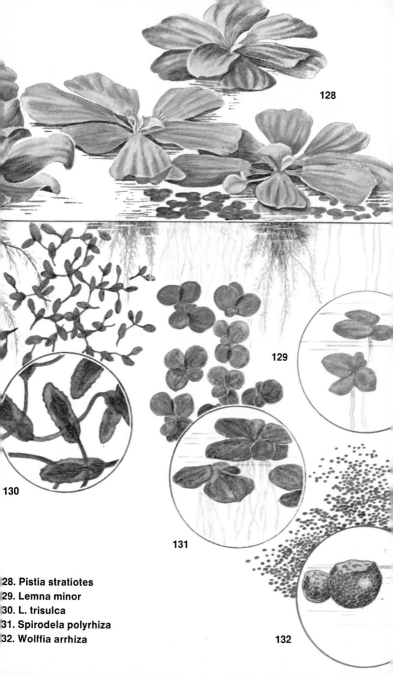

128

129

130

131

132

28. Pistia stratiotes
29. Lemna minor
30. L. trisulca
31. Spirodela polyrhiza
32. Wolffia arrhiza

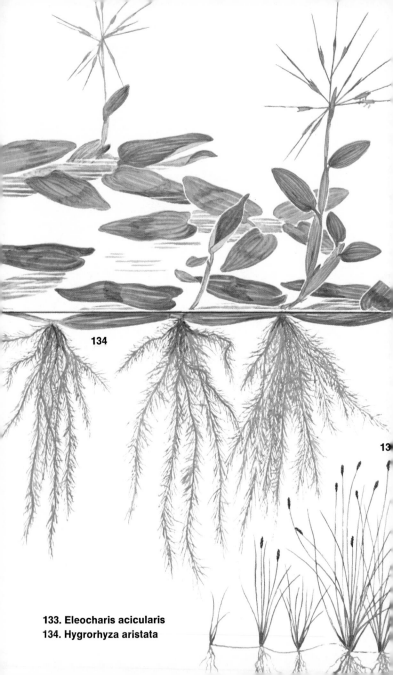

133. Eleocharis acicularis
134. Hygrorhyza aristata

Description of the Plants

Plants illustrated in the colour plates are indicated by a **bold** numeral.

Ricciaceae

Riccia fluitans **1**
Crystalwort
Cosmopolitan. A liverwort with branched thalli which floats just below the water surface, forming large dense mats. The light, water temperature and composition are not critical. This plant can also grow emerse if the conditions are sufficiently damp. Temperature (10-) 18-25°C.

Ricciocarpus natans **2**
Cosmopolitan. A liverwort with broad, branched thalli floating on the water surface, where it forms compact mats. There are long reddish-violet scales on the underside. This plant requires good light and a water rich in nutrients. Temperature (10-) 18-25°C.

Hypnaceae

Vesicularia dubyana **3**
Java Moss
South-east Asia. A moss with flat, much branched shoots which creeps horizontally or grows up into the water. It attaches itself to rocks or tree roots by rhizoids which arise on the underside of the stems. The emerse form is creeping. In the wild, this moss grows along the edges of shady rivers or on the bottom. It is one of the most rewarding aquarium plants, growing in soft or hard water, but good light is essential if it is to grow large. Temperature 18-28°C.

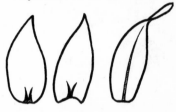

Leaves of (left to right) *Glossadelphus zolingeri*, *Vesicularia dubyana* and *Leptodictyum riparium* (×8).

Sematophyllaceae

Glossadelphus zollingeri
South-east Asia. A newly imported moss, similar to the preceding species, but with more rounded shoots and more upright growth.

Amblystegiaceae

Leptodictyum riparium **4**
Europe, Asia and North America. The submerse form of this moss has completely upright shoots and does not attach itself easily to the substrate. The leaves protrude obliquely or at right angles from the

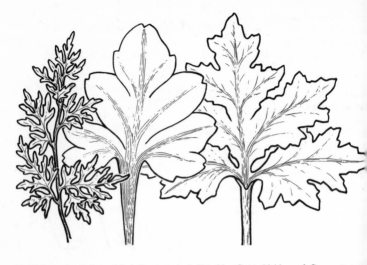

Leaf shape in (left to right) *Ceratopteris thalictroides*, *C. pteridoides* and *C. cornuta*.

stem. The emerse form is creeping with slightly flattened shoots and leaves that embrace the stem. This moss can be planted among rocks and roots in the aquarium. Temperature (10–) 18–25°C. Synonym *Amblystegium riparium*.

Parkeriaceae

Ceratopteris thalictroides   **5**
Floating Fern
South-east Asia and many other places. An aquatic fern which can grow to a height of more than 50 cm. The deeply divided leaves or fronds lie out over the water surface. The narrow spore-bearing leaves are erect and emerse, and the sori produce isospores. The plant reproduces vegetatively by means of numerous plantlets along the edges of the leaves. It grows submerse or at the surface. In the latter situation it forms an excellent aquarium plant with its long, finely divided roots hanging down in the water. When the plantlets are 5 10 cm across they can also be planted in the substrate. Temperature 20–22°C. There are about closely related species which are very difficult to distinguish from one another.

Ceratopteris cornuta
Africa. Leaves with only a few incisions and an angular, three

cornered outline. The petiole becomes only slightly broader at the leaf base.

Ceratopteris pteridoides
South America. Leaves with only a few incisions, but the triangular outline is more rounded. The petiole becomes much broader towards the leaf base.

Lomariopsidaceae

Bolbitis heudelotii **6**
Africa. A fern with a creeping rhizome and leaves 20-50 cm long. There are three leaf types: translucent green, coarsely toothed underwater leaves, broad, toothed emerse leaves and emerse spore-bearing leaves which are much narrower. The sori are in rows on the underside of these leaves, and they produce isospores. This form grows on rocks in rivers, often with *Anubias* (No. 101). It is rather difficult to keep in an aquarium tank. It must not be planted in the substrate but allowed to attach itself to a rock. Temperature 22-26°C. The water must not be too hard, and the lighting should be moderately bright. Propagation by division of the rhizome.

Bolbitis heteroclita **7**
South-east Asia. A fern with a creeping rhizome. The leaves usually have two side lobes. The sori are in groups on the underside of the leaves. Vegetative reproduction is by the formation of plantlets at the tip or edges of the leaves. In the wild this plant grows in damp, shady places with the leaves emerse. It is a more difficult plant to keep in the aquarium than the preceding species. Underwater it does not grow very large and the leaves become glassy green. Temperature 22-26°C. It should be allowed to attach itself to a rock or other firm object.

Polypodiaceae

Microsorium pteropus **8**
Java Fern
South-east Asia. A fern with a creeping rootstock and lanceolate leaves 10-30 cm long; in larger plants the leaves have one or two lateral lobes. The sori, arranged in groups on the underside of the leaves, produce isospores. Small plants develop along the leaf edges and on the sori, often in large numbers. This plant grows on rocks in fast-flowing, often shady rivers. It is very rewarding in the aquarium, although not reaching its full size. It should not, of course, be planted in the substrate. Small plants can be removed from the parent plant as soon as they have formed roots. Fragments of broken leaves allowed to float in the water will produce numerous small plants. Temperature (22-) 26-28°C. There is also a form with very narrow leaves.

Marsileaceae

Rootstock creeping. Leaves linear and undivided or with two or four leaflets. Spores in special spore-cases at the base of the leaves. Macro- and microspores.

Pilularia globulifera **9**
Pillwort
Europe. The long, creeping rootstock produces simple, linear leaves 10-15 cm long. This plant grows in sandy places in lakes with very acid water. It does not do well at high temperatures. There are about 6 species of *Pilularia* distributed throughout temperate regions, but little is known of their cultivation in the aquarium.

Leaves of (left to right) *Marsilea drum mondii* and *Regnellidium diphyllum*.

Marsilea hirsuta **10**
Australia. The submerse form has a tendency to produce long runners which often grow upwards in the water. The emerse form has short internodes and produces spore-bearing bodies. In the wild this plant grows along rivers and in lakes, often in large numbers. It requires plenty of light. Temperature 20-26°C.

The genus contains about 65 species from the warmer parts of the world, and is characterized by the four leaflets, but the species are rather difficult to distinguish from one another. *M. crenata* and *M. drummondii* are sometimes available on the market.

Regnellidium diphyllum
Brazil. Similar to the preceding species but the leaves have only two leaflets. The rootstock is somewhat longer.

Salviniaceae

Heterosporous ferns floating at the surface. The leaves grow in groups of three, two of which float above the surface, while one is submerse and root-like. The spore-cases develop on the submerse leaves and produce macro- and microspores. These plants require plenty of light and a water rich in nutrients if they are to thrive. When grown under good conditions they have an upright luxuriant growth and the species are easy to distinguish from one another. In poor conditions growth is inhibited and the leaves become small and rounded and almost the same for all the species. The upperside of the leaves is hairy and unwettable. Most of the species come from South America but some have spread to other tropical regions, becoming a serious pest in parts of the Indian sub-continent and south-eastern Africa.

Salvinia natans **11**
Water Velvet
Mediterranean area and Asia. Leaves 1 cm long. This plant should be overwintered at a somewhat lower temperature than the next species.

Salvinia auriculata **12**
South America. Leaves 2-3 cm long, brownish-green and somewhat sinuous. This plant requires good light and water rich in nutrients. It will then cover large areas of the water surface. Temperature 22-30°C.

Leaves of *Salvinia cucullata* and *S. oblongifolia*.

Salvinia oblongifolia
Brazil. The leaves are 5-10 cm long, and in fact several times longer than broad.

Salvinia cucullata
South-east Asia. Characterized by the cornet-shaped leaves which have a diameter of 1-2 cm.

Azollaceae

Azolla caroliniana **13**
Lesser Fairy Moss
America. Small, branched, bluish-green water ferns which float at the surface. The small leaves are overlapping. The lower leaf lobes contain blue-green algae which are responsible for the bluish coloration. These algae (*Anabaena azollae*) fix atmospheric nitrogen, which is thus available to the *Azolla*, while the latter shelters the algae and possibly also provides them with carbohydrates. Macro- and micro-spores are produced but these are of no importance in the aquarium where vegetative reproduction should be sufficient. With good light this species may form a thick carpet over the water surface in an aquarium.

Two other species, *A. pinnata* (South-east Asia) and *A, filiculoides* (South America) are also sometimes cultivated in the aquarium. (NB The Latin name is incorrectly spelt on the colour plate caption.)

Cabombaceae

CABOMBA

An American genus with 6 species. The plants have opposite much divided underwater leaves and rounded or sagittate floating leaves. Growing in slow-flowing rivers, canals and small lakes where the stems twist in and out among other vegetation. Cuttings do not always root easily, so it is better to bury the lower part of the stem horizontally so that 2-3 internodes are at a depth of 1-2 cm in the substrate.

Cabomba piauhyensis **14**
Central and South America. Leaves reddish, those underwater much incised, while the floating leaves are sagittate or narrow rhomboidal. Flowers reddish-violet. This plant

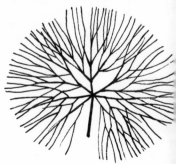

Leaves of *Cabomba caroliniana, C. piauhyensis* and *C. aquatica* (from above).

is difficult to keep in poor light. Temperature 22-26°C.

Cabomba caroliniana **15**
Carolina Water Shield
Southern North America. Leaves green, those underwater often with distinctly flattened leaf segments which are not so incised as in the preceding species. The floating leaves are sagittate. Flowers white. This plant can be cultivated for a long period at a temperature of 22-24°C, but overwintered at 18°C. (NB The Latin name is incorrectly spelt on the colour plate caption.)

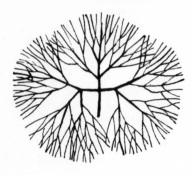

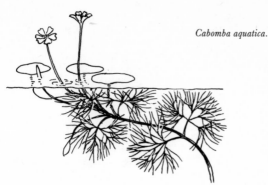

Cabomba aquatica.

Cabomba aquatica

Northern South America. Leaves green, often with a reddish tinge, and even more incised than those of No. 14. Floating leaves large and round. Flowers yellow. Temperature 22-26°C.

Nymphaeaceae

Stem in the form of a submerged corm or rhizome. Leaves submerged, floating and aerial. Flowers large with numerous petals, stamens and carpels. The seeds germinate readily.

NUPHAR

Rhizome stout, lying horizontally in the surface layer of the substrate. Flowers yellow, each petal bearing a nectary, stamens numerous. Fruit pea-shaped. This plant thrives best if the substrate is enriched.

Nuphar japonicum **16**

Japan, and cultivated in parts of south-east Asia. Underwater leaves 10-25 cm long, broad, sagittate and pale green with characteristic glassy markings. Floating leaves rounded sagittate. Temperature 22-26°C.

This is the most suitable *Nuphar* species for the tropical aquarium, and it grows best in slightly acid water.

Nuphar lutea **17**
Yellow Waterlily
Europe, North Asia and North America. Similar to the preceding species but with round leaves. This species is mainly marketed as seedlings as these are more tolerant of high temperatures. Mature specimens become very leggy at high temperatures and they often decay.

Nuphar pumilum
Europe and North Asia. Similar to the preceding species but smaller, and more tolerant of high temperatures.

Nuphar sagittifolium
Eastern North America. Similar to No. 16 but the leaves are twice as long and not curled.

NYMPHAEA

A genus with 20-30 species distributed throughout most of the world. Rootstock creeping or corm-like. Flowers with numerous, often coloured petals and numerous stamens. Only a few species are suitable for aquarium use. Some can be cultivated in outdoor ponds.

Nymphaea lotus group This group of waterlilies contains the closely related *N. pubescens* and *N. rubra* from Asia and *N. lotus* and *N. zenkeri* from Africa. Their systematic relationships are still not fully understood. The species are characterized by the numerous broad petals. The stamens are rounded and without a sterile appendage at the tip. The floating leaves have a characteristic toothed edge. The rootstock is short and corm-like. After overwintering the tip of the rootstock produces short runners which take root and form a further corm-like rootstock in the following year.

Nymphaea pubescens **18**
South-east Asia. The underwater leaves are reddish to greenish, sagittate to round. Floating leaves oval and up to 45 cm in length. Flowers white to pale red, 15-25 cm in diameter. Growing in large or small lakes and in canals. When put into water the dried corms sprout very rapidly and the fifth, sixth or seventh leaf usually reaches the surface. Under poor conditions the leaves remain small and only a few are floating. If planted in mud they quickly send up floating leaves and flower in the course of a couple of months. Large specimens can cover a couple of square metres of surface. Regular pruning will keep them submerse but they will then develop into small undernourished forms. Temperature 23-28°C. The flowers open at night. Synonym *N. 'stellata'*.

Nymphaea rubra
South-east Asia. The leaves are similar to those of the preceding species but more reddish. The flowers are large and they too are redder. There is no doubt that the two species are closely related and the present form is possibly only a cultivated, red-flowered variety of *N. pubescens*. It is found particularly in ponds close to buildings.

Nymphaea zenkeri **19**
Central West Africa. Mainly with underwater leaves which are green to red-brown with reddish-violet

markings. Flowers white. Growing in slow-flowing rivers in the rainforest, this plant is best kept at a temperature of 22-25°C, preferably with some nutrient in the substrate. Only a few floating leaves are formed. The plant often reaches a height of 40 cm, with a similar diameter. This is the best species of *Nymphaea* for aquarium use. It is closely related to *N. lotus* and is possibly to be regarded as a variety adapted to growing in running water.

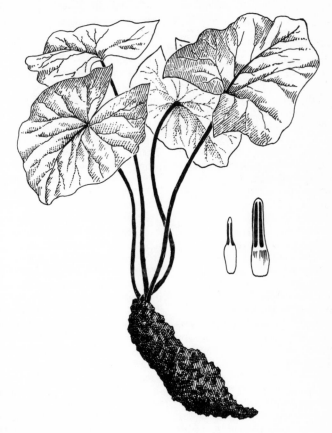

Nymphaea stellata and (left to right) stamens of *N. stellata* and *N. pubescens*.

Nymphaea lotus

Africa, growing in lakes, often those with muddy bottoms. The plant is characterized by the numerous round floating leaves and the white flowers. It is rarely imported. The leaves are almost all floating and the plant is therefore difficult to keep in an aquarium tank.

Nymphaea stellata group

Contains about 6 species from Africa and one from Asia. They are characterized by the fir-cone shape of the rootstock, the entire or roundly toothed leaves and the sterile appendage at the tip of each stamen.

Nymphaea stellata

Tropical Asia. Rootstock up to 10 cm long and 2 cm thick. Underwater leaves round and reddish. Floating leaves with roundly toothed edges and often with violet markings; the undersides are more or less violet. Flowers small, 5-13 cm across, whitish, pale red or bluish. Stamens 35-55, petals 11-14. Growing in lakes and canals. This species may be rather difficult to keep in the aquarium as it has a tendency to produce floating leaves. It requires good light and a substrate rich in nutrients. Temperature 22-28°C.

Nymphaea capensis

Southern and East Africa. Rootstock short. Closely related to the preceding form but usually with more blue in the flowers. Petals 20-30, stamens 150-275.

Nymphaea coerulea

Northern and Central Africa. Similar to the preceding species but the leaves are entire or slightly wavy, often with numerous markings on the underside. Petals 14-20, stamens 50-75. Easily propagated by seed.

Nymphaea heudelotii

Central West Africa. Closely related to the preceding species and possibly only a variety of it from running water.

Barclaya longifolia   **20**

Thailand. Rootstock narrow and ovate. The leaves have a characteristic opalescent sheen, and they vary from green to reddish, usually with conspicuous nerves. The flowers are greenish outside and dark red inside. The petals sit on top of the ovary and they never turn back completely. Self-pollination occurs quite frequently and with patience it is possible to germinate the seeds and produce large plants. This species grows in slow-flowing rivers in the rain-forest, often in waters containing iron. In the aquarium the best results are obtained by planting rootstocks which have just started to sprout. These should be planted 1 cm below the surface of the substrate, and in the course of a month or two the plant should be 50 cm tall and about the same in diameter. However, this ize will only be attained if the plant is grown in good light, at a temperature of 22-26°C, in water with added nutrient. After the plant has been in leaf for about 6 months it will die back, but will have formed one or more new rootstocks. About 6 months later these will start to sprout. This resting period often occurs over autumn or winter.

There are several other species of *Barclaya*, but they are very delicate and more difficult to keep in the aquarium.

Ceratophyllaceae

Ceratophyllum demersum **21**
Hornwort
Cosmopolitan. This plant hardly forms roots and mostly floats free in

the water or just below the surface. The fruit has three long spines. The very small male and female flowers are situated in the leaf axils. The leaves are arranged in whorls and much incised. The rather thick, hard leaf segments have tiny spines on the underside. A somewhat variable species found in all parts of the world. Plants from temperate regions do not thrive in tropical tanks as the temperature is too high. Those from the tropics do well at 22-28°C. They must have good light.

Ceratophyllum submersum
Cosmopolitan. Similar to the preceding species, but the leaves are thinner with fewer spines. The fruit lacks the long spines of *C. demersum*.

Leaf whorls of *Ceratophyllum demersum* and *C. submersum*.

Saururaceae

Saururus cernuus **22**
America. A marsh plant with stout runners which grows to a height of 50-75 cm. The inflorescence has small, stalked flowers, which have 6 stamens, but no petals or sepals. Growing in marshy places near rivers and lakes. In the aquarium this plant only reaches a height of 10-15 cm. It can be propagated by division of the long runners between the nodes. The pieces are then planted in a pot with damp soil and placed in a light position. They quickly sprout and after they have formed a couple of leaves they can be planted out in the aquarium. Temperature 20-26°C. There is a hairy form with pointed leaves and a smooth form with blunter leaves.

Amaranthaceae

Alternanthera reineckii **23**
South America. A marsh plant, growing to a height of 10-30 cm, with bronze-brown leaves which are reddish on the underside. The small, whitish flowers are grouped together in the upper leaf axils.

Leaf pairs of *Alternanthera reineckii* and *A. sessilis*.

They have 5 perianth segments and a few stamens. When kept in slightly acid water with good lighting this plant grows well but the internodes become very short and the leaves more reddish. For submerse culture it is best to plant seedlings. This species is characterized by the stems being hairy all round. Temperature 20-26°C. There are several forms of this species.

Alternanthera sessilis
Pantropical. A plant with longer, narrower leaves than the preceding species. The form cultivated in the aquarium has wine-red leaves. However it does not grow well in the aquarium. The stem has hairs arranged in longitudinal stripes.

Brassicaceae

Cardamine lyrata **24**
North-east Asia and Japan. A marsh plant with leaves in a rosette and a central inflorescence. The flowers have 4 sepals and 4 petals. Runners 20-40 cm long grow out from the rosette and these are suitable for planting in the aquarium. The leaves are lyre-shaped with 1-3 small pinnae. Roots form at each node. An undemanding plant which must, however, have good light. Temperature 18-20 (-22)°C.

Elatinaceae

Elatine macropoda **25**
Southern Europe. A small plant with opposite leaves and a creeping stem. The flowers are inconspicuous, with the parts arranged in fours (tetramerous). This plant should be placed in the foreground of the aquarium and the substrate should not be too coarse. A small amount of nutrient and good lighting are recommended. Temperature 18-22°C.

Primulaceae

Flowers usually pentamerous, with radial symmetry. Fruit capsules with one cell containing several ovules.

Samolus parviflorus **26**
America. The pale green, spatulate leaves grow in a rosette, and the central, branched inflorescence has numerous small white flowers. The marsh form flowers when the daylength exceeds 12 hours. Propagation is by seeds which germinate rapidly. In the wild this plant grows in muddy, marshy places, often in running water. It usually lives for a long time in the aquarium but it must have good light. Temperature 20-24°C. Synonym *S. floribundus.*

Hottonia palustris **27**
Water Violet
Europe. Leaves deeply pinnatisect. Flowers pale purple in whorls on a long erect flower stem. Growing in small lakes and canals. For the aquarium it is best to take small

Hottonia inflata.

side shoots and plant them as cuttings. Temperature 18-20°C. This
plant does best in very acid water,
not too rich in nutrient, with
moderate lighting.

Hottonia inflata
South-eastern North America. The
leaves are similar to those of the
preceding species but the flower
stems are much thickened and the
flowers small. This is a more suitable plant for the aquarium than
No. 27. Temperature 20-24
(-26)°C.

Euphorbiaceae

Phyllanthus fluitans **28**
Northern South America. Floating
plants with peculiar velvety-green
to reddish leaves with conspicuous
nerves. Flowers small and whitish.
Growing in small pools together
with *Azolla*, *Salvinia* and *Ricciocarpus*. In the aquarium it requires
good light and water rich in nutrients. Temperature (20-) 22-26°C.

Crassulaceae

Crassula helmsii **29**
Australia. Stems creeping with
erect branches (10-30 cm tall) and
opposite leaves. Flowers small, tetramerous, in the leaf axils. Growing
along rivers and in marshland,
often in dense masses. This is a good
plant for the foreground of an
aquarium tank, although it does
not grow fast. Temperature (17-)

20-26°C. Synonym   *C. recurva.*

Droseraceae

A small family with about 3 genera
of aquatic and marsh plants. They
all catch insects or other small invertebrates with specially modified
leaves.

Aldrovanda vesiculosa   **30**
Europe, Asia and Australia. The
plant is rootless and it floats just
below the surface. The leaves are in
whorls, each leaf consisting of two
semicircular lobes flanked by 4-6
bristles. The lobes are used to catch
small aquatic animals. The inside
of each lobe is furnished with hairs
and when these are touched the
lobes close together and entrap the
animal. The flowers are solitary in
the leaf axils. This is a difficult
plant to keep in the aquarium. It
requires good light. Temperature
18-22 (-24)°C.

Lythraceae

A family of mainly marsh and
meadow plants, some of which can
be cultivated in the aquarium.
Propagation is by cuttings. The
plants should be pruned when they
reach the water surface.

Didiplis diandra **31**
North America. Stems creeping
and erect, 5-15 cm. The opposite
leaves are narrow and ovate when
emerse, linear when submerse. In

good light this plant acquires a reddish sheen. The flowers are tetramerous and solitary in the leaf axils. Growing in damp places near rivers and lakes, often forming extensive carpets. In the aquarium it does well at a temperature of 22-26°C, in a substrate that is not too coarse. Synonym *Peplis diandra*.

Rotala macrandra **32**

India and Indo-China. The opposite leaves are 3 cm long, 1·5 cm broad, thin, reddish and greenish when submerse, and the emerse leaves are similar to those of the following species but twice as long. This is not an easy plant to grow in the aquarium. It requires slightly acid water, good light and a substrate rich in nutrient. Temperature 22-28°C.

Rotala rotundifolia **33**

South-east Asia. Emerse leaves are opposite, round and green, submerse are opposite or in a whorl of three, ovate to oblong, about 1 cm long and somewhat reddish. The flowers are small with fused sepals and violet petals. Temperature (18-) 22-28°C. This is a fast-growing plant in the aquarium, but sensitive to unfavourable conditions, when it will react by producing smaller leaves.

R. indica is to be regarded as a slightly larger form of *R. rotundifolia*.

Hydrolythrum wallichii

South-east Asia. Leaves reddish, linear, 1-2 cm long, arranged in whorls. Flowers reddish, in the leaf axils. Growing in canals and ponds, this plant requires good lighting

Hydrolythrum wallichii.

and very acid water rich in nutrients. Temperature 22-28°C. This is often a difficult plant to keep in the aquarium. Synonym *Rotala wallichii*.

Ammania senegalensis
Africa. Leaves opposite, 2-5 cm long, greenish to pale red-brown. Flowers reddish, in small groups in the upper leaf axils. Growing emerse and submerse in marshland, lakes and ponds. The submerse leaves are often longer, narrower and darker than the emerse. There are various forms of this species, not all of which are suitable for aquarium cultivation. Temperature 22-26°C. The lighting must be good.

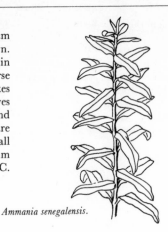

Ammania senegalensis.

Onagraceae

A family with many water and marsh plants. The genus *Ludwigia* (*Jussiaea*) contains several marsh plants, a few of which are cultivated in the aquarium. They can be propagated by cuttings. The flowers are bisexual and tetramerous.

Ludwigia repens **34**
Eastern North America. Leaves opposite, spatulate, 2-3 cm long, dark green above, green to wine-red below. The flowers, which have small yellow petals, are solitary in the leaf axils. This is an excellent undemanding plant for the aquarium. It requires good light. Temperature (15-) 20-24°C. Synonym *L. natans*.

Ludwigia arcuata **35**
South-eastern North America. Leaves opposite, 1-2 cm long, often with a reddish tinge. Emerse leaves are ovate, submerse linear or lanceolate. Flowers large and yellow. This plant can be cultivated like the preceding species, but is sometimes more difficult to keep in the aquarium.

Haloragaceae
MYRIOPHYLLUM

A cosmopolitan genus of aquatic plants, known as milfoils, with about 40 species. The submerse leaves are deeply incised and arranged in whorls. Emerse leaves are opposite or in whorls, often toothed.

he flowers are small and usually etramerous, in the leaf axils on merse shoots. Most of the species an be kept at 20-26°C, but some ill tolerate lower temperatures. Propagation is by cuttings. The ubstrate should be sand or gravel vith some added nutrient. Most pecies thrive in hard water, and hey must all have plenty of light.

Myriophyllum aquaticum **36**
North and South America, introduced in Asia. The emerse form has tout, stiff shoots with pale blue-green, finely incised leaves. The submerse form is more slender, with pale green leaves. Synonym *M. brasiliense.*

Myriophyllum mattogrossense **37**
South America. Stems stiff, red-brown. Leaves stiff, dark green, often with a reddish tinge.

Myriophyllum hippuroides
North and Central America. Leaves larger than in the preceding species, very finely incised and with a pale brownish tinge.

Apiaceae

A large family with only a few marsh and aquatic plants, with pentamerous lowers arranged in umbels.

Hydrocotyle leucocephala **38**
South America. A creeping marsh plant, 10-20 cm tall, with kidney-shaped, bluntly toothed leaves. Flowers yellow in a terminal umbel. The creeping habit is not retained in the aquarium where the plant grows up to the light. Temperature 20-24°C.

Hydrocotyle verticillata **39**
North and Central America. A creeping plant, 10-15 cm tall, with peltate leaves. The flowers are in whorls up the stems. In the aquarium this species retains the creeping habit but grows more slowly. Temperature (15-) 20-24°C.

Lilaeopsis attenuata **40**
South America. Stem creeping with leaves and roots growing from each node. The emerse leaves are 3-8 cm long. Flowers in an umbel. Growing in damp places close to lakes, rivers and ditches. This plant has only recently been imported for the aquarium and there are possibly several species on the market. It thrives best when the water is not too hard. The substrate should not be coarse, and the addition of nutrient is recommended. There must be plenty of light. Temperature (18-) 20-24°C.

Menyanthaceae

Nymphoides indica **41**
Asia and Africa. The rootstock is
usually not buried in the substrate,
but is merely attached by a few
roots. The rounded leaves float at
the surface. This plant is peculiar
in that the flowers appear to arise
from the leaf stalk at some distance
below the leaf itself. The pentamerous flowers have white hairy petals.
Growing in muddy areas in lakes
and ponds where it is in full sun.
In the aquarium it requires very
good light, some nutrient and a
temperature of 22-28°C, but often
it does not live for very long.

The genus contains about 25
species, of which a few are occasionally available on the market.

Scrophulariaceae

A large family (about 200 genera) with a few aquatic representatives. The
flowers have tubular sepals and 2-4 stamens. The leaves are opposite or
in whorls.

Hydrotriche hottoniiflora **42**
Madagascar. The submerse leaves
are linear and arranged in whorls.
The stems are more or less branched
and often very long. The flowers
have a pale blue marking on the
corolla. Found in slow-flowing
waters, this plant requires water
rich in nutrients and plenty of light.
It is not always easy to cultivate in
the aquarium. Temperature 20-
24°C.

Bacopa caroliniana **43**
North America. 10-20 cm tall with
cordate, hairy, dark green leaves.
Flowers blue, with 4 stamens.
Growing in marshy places. In the
aquarium this plant does not grow
as large as it does in the wild and
the leaves become smaller and
more rounded. Temperature (18-)

22-26°C. Synonym *B. amplexi-
caule.*
(NB The Latin name is incorrectly
spelt on the colour plate caption.)

Bacopa rotundifolia
North America. Similar to the preceding species but with a white
marking on the corolla. The leaves
are larger, pale green and more
rounded. This plant does not thrive
so well in the aquarium as No. 43.

Bacopa monnieri **44**
Pantropical. Leaves smooth and
spatulate. Flowers small, blue, with
short stalks. Found growing near
coasts, in shore meadows and in the
inner mangrove zone. When cultivated underwater the leaves become very round, and growth is
slower. Temperature 20-28°C.

Bacopa rotundifolia.

Lindernia rotundifolia   **45**
South-east Asia, India and Sri Lanka; introduced into America. A creeping marsh plant with roundish, opposite leaves. Flowers pentamerous with two stamens and white petals with blue markings. Found growing in sandy places in and along rivers. It is characteristic that roots grow out from the leaf axils. Temperature 20-26°C.

LIMNOPHILA
This genus contains about 35 species in Africa and Asia, of which a few are cultivated in the aquarium. The emerse leaves are often very different from the submerse. Flowers pentamerous with 4 stamens. The species described here are very similar to one another. The chromosome numbers further complicate the position for there are diploid, triploid and tetraploid plants. The basic chromosome number is 17. *L. aquatica* has $2n = 34$, while *L. sessiliflora* has 34 or 51, and *L. indica* 34 or 68 chromosomes. It is therefore possible that each species contains plants with 34, 51 or 68 chromosomes. Some plants, such as those with 51 chromosomes, are sterile but they reproduce vegetatively.

Limnophila aquatica   **46**
India and Sri Lanka. Submerse leaves much divided, emerse leaves opposite and toothed. Flower stalks 2-12 mm long. Flowers large, 8-13 mm long, with a mainly violet corolla. Found growing in slow-flowing rivers and canals, also in paddy fields. When growing well this is a very handsome plant with the whorls of submerse leaves attaining a diameter of 10-15 cm. To reach this size the plants must have good light and water rich in nutrient but without too much calcium. Temperature 22-26°C.

Limnophila sessiliflora   **47**
Southern and south-east Asia. The submerse leaves are not so finely divided as in No. 46. The emerse leaves are in whorls, and are sharply toothed or with only a few lobes. The flower stalk is short (0-1.5 mm). Flowers 8-10 mm long,

white with pale blue or violet markings. The plant branches repeatedly, forming dense aggregations which send roots down into the substrate. It may also produce stems that creep along the bottom. This species is not quite so demanding as No. 46 as regards light and nutrients.

Limnophila heterophylla
South-east Asia. Submerse leaves finely divided in whorls of 6-8, emerse leaves smaller, darker green and toothed, in whorls of 2-4. Flower stalk 0·5-2 mm long. Corolla 5-6 mm long, white with violet markings in the throat.

Limnophila indica
Africa, Asia and Australia. Submerse leaves finely divided, emerse lanceolate and toothed. Flower stalk 3-10 mm long, corolla 8-12 mm long, white to pale red. This plant smells like turpentine and the sap is poisonous to fishes. Synonym *L. gratioloides*.

Micranthemum umbrosum **48**
Eastern North America and South America. A small, creeping plant (5-15 cm) with opposite circular leaves. Flowers in the leaf axils, with a four-lobed calyx and two stamens. Found in shady places along the banks of rivers and lakes. A delicate plant which should be grown in a sandy substrate with added nutrient. It is avidly eaten by fishes. Temperature 20-24°C.

Lentibulariaceae

Utricularia gibba **49**
Pantropical. A rootless plant. Stems thin with few leaves and small bladders or vesicles which catch tiny aquatic invertebrates. The bladders have small trigger bristles. When these are touched by a small animal the valve of the bladder opens and the animal is sucked in. After some time inside the bladder the animal dies and is digested and the resulting material is taken up by the plant. The flowers are yellow and are produced on emerse stalks. An attractive and undemanding plant for the aquarium. Temperature 20-26°C.

Occasionally other larger species appear on the market but they are more difficult to keep for any length of time.

Acanthaceae

A large tropical family in which only one genus, *Hygrophila*, has plants suitable for the aquarium. Leaves opposite and more or less hairy. Flowers pentamerous, with an upper and lower lip, four stamens and two carpels. Found growing in damp places near lakes and rivers, or sometimes submerse. Propagation by cuttings. Single leaves that float will quickly form roots and new shoots.

Hygrophila polysperma: a torn-off leaf with a newly formed plant.

Hygrophila polysperma **50**
Bangladesh and Thailand. A creeping plant with narrow ovate, pale green to brownish-green leaves, 2–10 cm long. Flowers small and pale blue, in a terminal head. Temperature (18-) 22-26°C. One of the best plants for the aquarium, as it is undemanding, fast-growing and easy to propagate.

Hygrophila difformis **51**
India, Thailand and Malaya. Submerse leaves up to 10 cm long and pinnatifid, becoming ovate and toothed when growing emerse. The leaf shape depends in part upon the light conditions. Flowers large and blue, in the leaf axils. Found growing in canals and paddy fields. A good plant for the aquarium, but it requires bright light and a substrate rich in nutrients. Temperature 22-26°C. The variable leaf shape is a striking example of the variability of aquatic plants. Synonym *Synnema triflorum.*

Hygrophila guyanensis **52**
Northern South America. Leaves narrow to broadly lanceolate, 10–12 cm long. Flowers small, whitish, in the leaf axils. Found growing in damp places along the banks of lakes and ditches. In the aquarium this species is not particularly demanding, but it does best in good light. Temperature 20-24°C. A variable species, in which the leaf may be from 0·5 to 5 cm broad. A plant with a leaf breadth of 0·5 cm has been cultivated under the misleading appellation *H. salicifolia* (= *H. angustifolia*) which is actually the name of a species with very large red flowers which comes from Asia.

Hygrophila corymbosa **53**
Thailand. Leaves ovate, hairy, with a violet tinge and about 10 cm long.

Different leaf forms in *Hygrophila difformis*.

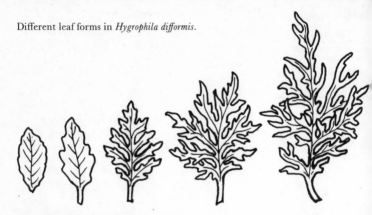

Submerse leaves very large and pale green. Flowers violet, in the leaf axils. Often growing as a weed in paddy fields, also in rivers and canals. This is a good plant for the aquarium but when grown in poor light it often loses the lower leaves. Synonyms *H. stricta* and *Nomaphila stricta*.

In recent years some forms resembling *H. corymbosa* have been found, but they have not yet been identified. Their growth is more compact and their submerse leaves are longer and narrower. Growth is slower and they do better underwater.

Hydrocharitaceae

A family with 15 genera, containing plants that are all aquatic. The flowers are bisexual or unisexual. Many have pollination mechanisms specially adapted for an aquatic environment. Some species, such as *Elodea canadensis*, *Egeria densa* and *Hydrilla verticillata*, have been distributed throughout the world by man and have become serious pests.

VALLISNERIA
Mainly tropics and subtropics. Leaves linear and radical. Separate male and female plants. Vegetative reproduction by runners. The female flowers are solitary on a long stalk which grows up to the surface. They have 3 petals and 3 sepals which open just above the water surface, and 3 styles each of which is split into two lobes. The male flowers have short stalks and are

Vallisneria gigantea: a female flower and two floating male flowers.

gathered several together in a spathe. These flowers are released from an opening at the top of the spathe and they float straight up to the surface. After a short time they open with the 3 sepals and 3 petals bending backwards so that the stamens (1-3) are raised slightly

above the water surface. These free, floating male flowers can then be blown about on the surface until they meet a female flower. After pollination the stalk of the female flower forms a spiral which takes the flower below the surface. In the wild, *Vallisneria* species grow in streams and small rivers, often in large populations. Temperature (18-) 22-28°C. The systematics of the genus are difficult, and it is not clear whether there are 6-8 species or possibly only 2-3.

Vallisneria gigantea **54**
New Guinea and the Philippines, and certainly introduced in other parts of Asia, and possibly elsewhere. Leaves up to 2 m long and 1-3 cm broad. Under aquarium conditions this plant is somewhat smaller and it only produces a few runners. It is often regarded as a form of *V. natans*.

Vallisneria natans var. *natans* **55**
South-east Asia. Leaves up to 1 m long and 3-4 cm broad. The rhizome is characteristically vertical. This is a most suitable plant for the aquarium. Synonym *V. asiatica* var. *asiatica*.

Vallisneria natans var. *biwaensis* **56**
South-east Asia. Similar to the preceding form, but the leaves are much twisted. It is sometimes difficult to keep. Synonym *V. asiatica* var. *biwaensis*.

Vallisneria gigantea with male inflorescences.

Vallisneria spiralis
Europe, Africa and Asia. Similar to
No. 55 but without the long vertical
rhizome. Some years ago *V. spiralis*
was the form usually grown in the
aquarium, but *V. natans* appears
gradually to have taken its place.

BLYXA

A genus of about 10 species from
Africa, Asia and Australia. Leaves
lanceolate, in radical rosettes arranged along the stem. The flowers
are unisexual or bisexual, the males
being stalked, the females and bi-
sexuals sessile. The species are best

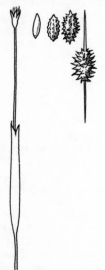

Flower of *Blyxa aubertii* and seeds (left to
right) of *B. japonica*, *B. aubertii*, *B.
octandra* and *B. echinosperma*.

identified by the appearance of the
seeds. Found growing in standing
or slow-flowing and often muddy
waters. Sometimes difficult to grow
in the aquarium. They require
good light, a substrate rich in
nutrient and a temperature of (22-)
24-28°C. A supplement of iron is
often necessary. In good light they
flower quite readily, and the leaves
become somewhat reddish. They
are easily propagated by seeds, but
the seedlings must be reared in a
separate tank until they are large
enough to plant out.

Blyxa aubertii   **57**
Asia to Australia. Leaves 10-70 cm
long. The flowers are bisexual and
self-pollination often occurs.

Blyxa echinosperma
South and East Asia. Similar to the
preceding species but often slightly
smaller. Easily recognized by the
spiny seeds.

Blyxa octandra
India to Australia. Leaves usually
20-30 cm long. Flowers on separate
male and female plants.

Blyxa japonica
South and East Asia. Leaves 2-5 cm
long, arranged along the 5-30 cm
long stem. The flowers are bisexual.
The branched stems break rather
easily, but if conditions are right
the broken-off pieces will root quite
quickly.

Flower of *Egeria densa.*

Egeria densa **58**

South America, and introduced in many other places. Leaves pale green, 1-2 cm long, in whorls of about 6 along the stem. Separate male and female flowers, with nectaries. The female flowers are solitary and grow up to the surface. The male flowers, also emerse, are in groups of 2-4. Found growing in lakes and slow-flowing rivers, rich in nutrient. They require good light and fairly hard water. Temperature 18-26°C. Under good conditions this species grows rapidly and requires regular pruning. Synonym *Elodea densa.*

Lagarosiphon muscoides **59**

Southern Africa. Leaves dark green, 1-2 cm long and much recurved, on

Male and female flower of *Lagarosiphon muscoides.*

long stems. Separate male and female plants, and the flowers lack nectaries. Female spathes are in the leaf axils, each containing 1-3

Female flower (left) and male flower of *Hydrilla verticillata.*

flowers. Male spathes contain numerous flowers which break off and float to the surface where they open. The three stamens project horizontally, while three structures known as staminodes rise vertically and act as sails. Found growing in

Female flower (left) and male flower of *Elodea canadensis.*

standing or slow-flowing waters. This plant usually grows rather slowly in the aquarium. It requires good light and water rich in nutrient. Temperature (18-) 20-24°C.

Hydrilla verticillata **60**

Africa to Asia. Leaves green, about 2 cm long, with toothed margins, in whorls of 6-8 on long stems. Separate male and female flowers. The female flowers are solitary and just reach to the surface where they form a 'saucer' which is water-repellent on account of its waxy coating. The male flowers, on short stalks, break loose and float to the surface where they open. The 3 petals and 3 sepals bend back and at the same time the 3 stamens do the same. The stamens suddenly spring up from this position and throw pollen in all directions, to a distance of about 15 cm. Some of the pollen will land on a female flower.

Found growing in standing or running waters. In the aquarium this plant grows quite rapidly, even with moderate lighting, and has to be regularly pruned. The stems tend to break very easily. Temperature (18-) 22-26°C. Synonym *H. lithuanica*.

Elodea canadensis **61**
Canadian Waterweed
North America, and introduced in many other places. Leaves about 1 cm long, in whorls of 3-5 along the stems. Flowers unisexual and solitary with a long perianth-tube which reaches the surface. The male and female flowers are similar in form to one another. Growing in standing or flowing waters, often those rich in nutrient or with a content of calcium. In the aquarium this plant grows well in good light and without too much heat. Temperature 15-21°C.

Limnobium spongia **62**
North America. A usually floating plant with a rosette of stalked, thick, cordate leaves with a diameter of 3-4 cm. Vegetative reproduction by runners 3-10 cm long. In the summer when the plant is growing well it forms large, spatulate aerial leaves. The flowers are unisexual with pointed perianth segments. Growing in lakes and slow-flowing waters, often in large masses in shallow areas. In the aquarium this is an excellent floating plant which produces numerous runners. It requires good lighting. Temperature 20-24°C.

Limnobium laevigatum **63**
South and Central America. Similar to the preceding species but the leaves are smaller, with shorter stalks, and closer to one another. The runners are 1-4 cm long. Synonym *L. stoloniferum*.

OTTELIA

A tropical genus with about 40 species, of which a few are suitable for the aquarium. The leaves are floating or submerse. The flowers are solitary or several together, and with three large petals. Propagation is by seeds which germinate readily. The plants require good light and a rich substrate.

Ottelia alismoides **64**
North-east Africa to south-east Asia and Australia. Leaves submerse,

Ottelia mesenterium.

talked and (10-) 20-40 cm long. Leaf blade green, roundish to cordate, but lanceolate when young. Flowers bisexual with 3 white petals which are yellow at the base. Fruit usually with 4-7 wings. This plant sets seed readily. Found growing in paddy-fields, canals and rivers with a muddy bottom. It may be difficult to establish in the aquarium, where it must first form new roots. It requires good light. Temperature 22-28°C.

Ottelia lanceolata

Indo-China. Similar to the preceding, but it may grow very large. Separate male and female plants. Fruit with 7-12 very large wings.

Ottelia ulvifolia **65**
Africa. Leaves dark brownish-green
to green, broad lanceolate, up to
40 cm long. Flowers bisexual,
yellow. Fruit with two wings. More
difficult to keep than the preceding
species, and the dark brown coloration only appears in good light. The
plant requires a rich substrate and
slightly acid water.

Ottelia cordifolia
India. Fully grown leaves are floating, 15-30 cm long. Leaf blade
ovate, 5-10 cm long. Flowers unisexual. Female flowers solitary,
male flowers several together.
Otherwise as for the preceding
species. Synonym *Bootia cordifolia.*

Ottelia mesenterium
Celebes. Leaves 15-25 cm long and
much curled. A difficult species to
cultivate.

Limnocharitaceae

Hydrocleis nymphoides **66**
South America. Stem creeping,
producing leaves and flowers from
the nodes. Leaf blade cordate on a
stalk 5-10 cm long. Flowers yellow
with violet stamens and only open
for one day. Growing in lakes and
slow-flowing rivers where it may
form dense masses. In the aquarium
it is not particularly demanding,
but it must have good light. An
excellent plant for an aqua-
vivarium. Temperature 20-26°C.

There are about 9 species of
Hydrocleis, but they are rarely seen
on the market.

Alismataceae

A family of about 10 genera with about 70 or more species, most of which
come from South and North America. They are mainly marsh plants. The
flowers have three green sepals and three petals.

ECHINODORUS

South America to North America.
About 45 species. Leaves narrow
lanceolate to broadly cordate, in
rosettes. The smallest species are
only a few centimetres tall, the
largest several metres. The leaf
stalk may be rounded or angular.

Leaf blades with curved nerves
ending at the tip; these nerves are
joined by a network of cross nerves.
For the reliable identification of the
species it is necessary to have
flowering specimens and preferably
also the fruits. The flowers are bisexual, in often branched inflorescences. The flower stalks may be

ounded, angular or winged. Stamens vary in number from 6 to numerous. Carpels numerous; the individual carpels are nutlets and when adult they have a characteristic pattern of ribs and glands. The nutlets often have a long beak. There is a short rhizome with long roots which anchor the plant in the substrate.

The large area of distribution means that the growing conditions vary considerably according to the species. Some almost always grow in marshland, e.g. *E. grandiflorus*. Others grow submerse for part of the year, e.g. *E. tenellus*, while some are permanently submerse. Some species grow in running water, others in lakes or marshes.

The identification of *Echinodorus* species, apart from the most common, is often very difficult. This is because of the great variation in form of the emerse and submerse leaves within a single species.

Most species of *Echinodorus* are very suitable for cultivation in the aquarium. Some become very large and may grow up above the water surface. This can be prevented by pruning the roots with a knife while they are still in the substrate, or by reducing the number of leaves. Growth can also be restricted by planting in pots.

For good growth the substrate should contain some nutrient (calcium-free) and preferably some sphagnum moss. The lighting should be good and the water

slightly acid. The addition of iron is often necessary; yellowing of the leaves usually means that the plants are deficient in iron.

Echinodorus can be propagated by seeds, but in the aquarium it is more usual to use the plantlets which form alongside or instead of the flowers.

Echinodorus tenellus　**67**
North to South America. Leaves lanceolate, up to 10-15 cm long. Runners 2-5 cm long. Submerse plants are smaller, with linear leaves. Flowers about 6 mm in diameter, a few in each inflorescence. This plant forms dense populations in lakes and flooded places near rivers. It is best cultivated in sand with some loam, and it must have good light. Temperature (15-) 20-26°C. Synonym *E. parvulus*.

Echinodorus magdalenensis　**68**
Dwarf Amazon Sword Plant
Tropical America. Leaves pale green, lanceolate, 5-10 cm long. Submerse leaves may grow to a length of 20-30 cm. Flowers about 1 cm across, in simple inflorescences. Growing in lakes and rivers. A rewarding aquarium plant which grows very rapidly and may form runners a metre long with small plants every 5-10 cm. These plantlets should be cut off and planted separately. Temperature (18-) 20-26°C. A common aquarium plant which over the years has

been grown under various names. Synonyms *E.* *'intermedius'*, *E.* *'grisebachii'* and *E.* *'latifolius'*.
(NB The Latin name is incorrectly spelt on the colour plate caption.)

Echinodorus major **69**
Brazil. Leaves usually pale green, leathery and smooth, with conspicuous broad, pale nerves, 15-40 cm long. Flowers borne on short stalks in an unbranched inflorescence. A most suitable plant for the aquarium as it does not form emerse leaves, but it requires good light and a rich substrate. Temperature (18-) 20-24°C. Synonym *E. martii.*

Echinodorus berteroi **70**
Cellophane Plant
Central to North America. Emerse leaves on long stalks with a cordate blade 5-10 cm long (No. 70a), floating leaves somewhat smaller. Submerse leaves 10-30 cm long, 2-4 cm broad, translucent green, with conspicuous nerves. Flowers in a large inflorescence. This plant can be propagated by seeds, or by taking the small plants that form on the rhizome. In the aquarium it can be kept submerse if the floating leaves are cut off. It dies back in the winter. Temperature (18-) 20-24°C. Synonyms *E. rostratus* and *E. 'cordifolius'.*

Echinodorus bleheri **71**
Southern Brazil. Leaves lanceolate, 30-50 cm long, often with a characteristic network of nerves. This species, which seldom flowers, grows in sandy substrates in slow flowing rivers. It does well in the aquarium when there is some nutrient in the substrate. Yellowing of the leaves is usually a sign of iron deficiency. Temperature (18-) 20-26°C. Synonym *E. 'paniculatus'.*

E. amazonicus
Southern Brazil. Similar to the preceding species, but smaller and with narrower leaves, which are often recurved. A very common aquarium plant. Synonym *E. 'brevipedicellatus'.*

Echinodorus osiris **72**
Southern Brazil. Emerse leaves (No. 72a) elliptical, sometimes reddish. Submerse leaves oblong with conspicuous nerves. This plant is often rough owing to the presence of small, stiff siliceous formations. It requires good light and a substrate rich in nutrients. Temperature (16-) 20-24°C. Synonyms *E. 'longistylis'* and *E. 'rubra'.*

Echinodorus macrophyllus **73**
Brazil. Leaves up to 1·5 m long, leaf blades cordate, up to 30 cm long. Inflorescence branched, up to 2 m tall. Plants form on the inflorescence. This species has characteristic outgrowths (10 ×2 mm) on the lateral roots. It grows in marshy places. In the aquarium it can be kept submerse, but will then require regular pruning. Synonyms *E. 'cordifolius'* and *E. 'radicans'.*

Echinodorus horemanii **74**
Southern Brazil. Leaves lanceolate,
30-40 cm long, smooth, translucent, deep green with broad
nerves. Similar to No. 69, but the
leaf stalks are longer and the leaf
blades more translucent. It requires good light and a rich substrate. Temperature (16-) 20-
24°C. Synonym *E. 'undulatus'*.

Echinodorus horizontalis **75**
Peru, Colombia and Brazil. Leaf
blade 10-20 cm long, pointed
cordate. It is characteristic that the
leaf blade is usually at an angle to
the stalk, so that it lies horizontally
in the water. This is a marsh plant
which is rather difficult to keep in
the aquarium as it has a tendency
to decay. Temperature 22-26°C.

Echinodorus palaefolius var.
latifolius **76**
Brazil. Leaves up to 1 m long, leaf
blades up to 25 cm, broad ovate,
pointed. Inflorescence 1·5 m tall,
branched, its stalk with conspicuous wings. Flowers stalked. Plantlets are formed on the inflorescence.
This is a marsh plant which grows
in muddy places in rivers. It is very
suitable for the aquarium, where it
does not grow too large, the submerse leaves becoming narrower.
Temperature 20-26°C.

Echinodorus palaefolius var.
palaefolius
Leaves up to 50 cm long with a
more cordate blade than in the

preceding form. Flowers not
stalked.

Echinodorus subalatus **77**
Central to South America. Leaves
up to 50 cm long, the blade ovate
with a decurrent base (running
down the stem). Inflorescence unbranched or with a few branches.

Echinodorus cordifolius **78**
North to South America. Leaves up
to 60 cm long, leaf blades 20-30 cm,
rounded cordate. Inflorescence unbranched or with a few branches,
often nodding, with plantlets at the
nodes. Found growing in lakes and
rivers, this is an attractive plant for
the aquarium but it may be difficult
to establish. Temperature 20-24°C.

SAGITTARIA

North and South America, Europe
and south-east Asia. A genus with
about 20 species, most of which
occur in America. The leaves are
variable in shape: submerse leaves
linear, floating leaves cordate, ovate
or linear, and emerse leaves linear
to sagittate. The runners often swell
up at the tip to form an overwintering corm. Flowers trimerous in a
simple or tufted inflorescence; the
lower flowers usually female, the
upper ones male. Several carpels,
each with a short curved beak.

The species of *Sagittaria* grow in
lakes and slow-flowing rivers, where
the plants are well anchored. Only
a few North American species are

grown in the aquarium, where they should have good lighting and a substrate of sand mixed with a little loam.

Sagittaria subulata var. *subulata* **79**
North and South America. Leaves linear, up to 30 cm long and 1-6 mm broad. Floating and emerse leaves often with an ovate blade. In this and the other subspecies the female flower stalks bend backwards when the fruits are ripening and the stamens are hairless. Temperature (15-) 19-24°C. Synonyms *S. natans*, *S. lorata*, *S. pusilla*, *S. subulata* var. *pusilla* and *S. natans* var. *lorata*.

Sagittaria subulata var. *gracillima*
North America. Similar to the preceding, but the leaves are up to 1 m long and 1-3 mm broad. Synonyms *S. natans* var. *gracillima* and *S. filiformis*.

Sagittaria subulata var. *kurziana*
Florida. Similar to the two preceding plants, but the leaves are 1-3 m long and 7-14 mm broad. Synonym *S. kurziana*.

Sagittaria graminea var. *graminea* **80**
North America. Leaves up to 40 cm long and 1 cm broad. The emerse leaves may be lanceolate. In this form the female flowers do not bend backwards after flowering and the stamens are hairy. This is the commonest form grown in the aquarium. Temperature 19-24°C. Syno-

nyms *S. eatonii* and *S. isoetiformis*.
Sagittaria graminea var.
platyphylla **81**
Similar to No. 80, but the submerse leaves are up to 1·5 cm broad. The stalks of the female flowers may bend backwards after flowering. Synonym *S. platyphylla*.

Sagittaria graminea var. *teres*
Leaves circular, 5-15 cm across. Synonym *S. teres*.

Aponogetonaceae
APONOGETON

A genus with about 45 species in Africa (13), Madagascar (11), south-east Asia (9), New Guinea (2) and Australia (4). With a rhizome or tuber. Leaves linear or stalked with a blade. Flowers usually bisexual, in the leaf axils, and surrounded by a spathe which usually falls off. Perianth with (1-) 2 (3-6) segments. Stamens 6 or more. Carpels (2-) 3 (4-9). Most of the species can only be propagated by seeds, which are usually produced when the inflorescence is pollinated by a brush (self-pollination). When the seeds are ripe the carpel disintegrates and the seeds float at the water surface. Later on they sink to the bottom, by which time they will already have germinated. Flowering and seed production occurs very commonly in the aquarium.

The species are found in lakes and rivers from sea level to altitudes f 2,000 m, in acid, neutral or alkaline water. The water temperature varies from 15 to 30°C according to the species, and the substrate from mud to sand and gravel. Many species are excellent aquarium plants which with care may be kept for several years. However, some die quite quickly on account of poor conditions or simply because they are not suitable for the aquarium.

In the aquarium the substrate should preferably consist of sand or gravel with some loam. The rootstock should not be planted too deep, but only just covered. Most species should be given a resting period of 2-5 months in the year. As a rule the resting period starts in early winter when the plant, which has been large and luxuriant, suddenly loses its leaves and becomes smaller. The aquarist can then either lower the temperature by 2-4°C, or he can remove the rootstock and keep it cool, at a temperature of (15-) 18-20°C, and slightly damp, but not wet. It should be kept in a mixture of quartz sand and loam with a little sphagnum moss. After a few months it can be put back in the aquarium where it will soon sprout.

The African species are not described here as they have not been much used in the aquarium.

Aponogeton rigidiflorus 82
Sri Lanka. Rhizome horizontal, creeping, 0·5–1·0 cm across. Leaves 10–100 cm long, leathery, brownish-green, the younger ones reddish, and curled at the edges. Inflorescence unbranched, at first nodding. Found growing in slow-flowing waters in the south-western rain-forest, often together with *Blyxa* (No. 57). In the aquarium this plant requires good light and some nutrient, together with iron, but it is not easy to keep. Temperature 22–26°C. This is one of the species which does not require a resting period.

Aponogeton crispus 83
Sri Lanka. Rhizome vertical, 1–2 cm across. Leaves up to 50 cm long, green to brown. Leaf blade 10–20 cm long, 3–5 cm across, with a broad base and rounded tip. Leaf

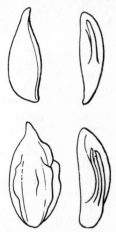

Fruit and seed of (above) *Aponogeton crispus* and *A. echinatus* (×3).

edge slightly curled to wavy. Inflorescence unbranched, at first nodding. Fruits smooth. Growing in rivers and lakes up to an altitude of 2,000 m, at temperatures of 15 to 25°C. An undemanding plant which does well in the aquarium if given a little loam in the substrate. It tolerates bright light.

There are two varieties, the relationships of which are not known. In lowland plants the leaves are more pointed and some may be floating (thus resembling No. 84), while plants from greater altitudes have more rounded, often shorter leaves, which may be red-brown.

Aponogeton echinatus **84**

Southern India. Rhizome up to 1·5 cm thick. Submerse leaves 20–50 cm long, 1–2 cm across, lanceolate, often with a brownish-green tinge, the edges very wavy. Floating leaves lanceolate, without wavy edges, and produced after the submerse leaves. Inflorescence unbranched, at first nodding. Fruits uneven, with irregular surfaces. Growing in muddy places in lakes and canals, this is one of the best species of *Aponogeton* for aquarium cultivation. It requires bright light and a rich substrate. Temperature (18-) 22-28°C. It is advisable to give this species a resting period. The floating leaves should be cut off to encourage the submerse leaves. Propagation by seed is not difficult. For many years this species has been cultivated under the name '*A. crispus*'.

Aponogeton natans **85**

India and Sri Lanka. Rhizome somewhat irregularly rounded. Leaves floating and lanceolate with a cordate base. Inflorescence unbranched, erect, bluish. Growing in lakes and slow-flowing rivers. In the aquarium this plant should be given good light and a rich substrate and it requires a resting period. Temperature 22-28°C.

Aponogeton ulvaceus **86**

Madagascar. Rhizome more or less horizontal, up to 3 cm across, and somewhat rough. Leaves 30-50 (-100) cm long, pale green, brownish when grown in bright light, and slightly translucent. Leaf blade 15-30 cm long, 2-8 cm across with very wavy edges, causing the whole leaf to become twisted. The flowering stem ends in twin spikes 6-8 cm long. Growing in standing to fast-flowing, sometimes alkaline waters. In the aquarium this species does well when grown in good light and a rich substrate. Temperature (18-) 20-24°C. A resting period is required. The flowers cannot be self-pollinated.

Aponogeton undulatus **87**

India to Thailand and Malaysia. Rhizome short, about 1 cm across. Leaves 20-60 cm long, 1-4 cm across, somewhat wavy with translucent chequered green coloration. Inflorescence unbranched with very large, spatulate perianth segments. Instead of the inflorescence, plantlets, usually 2-4 in a row, often

Aponogeton lakhonensis.

develop on the stalk. These can be planted out when the stalk withers. Growing in ponds and canals, this is a good, adaptable plant for the aquarium, where it should be given a resting period. Temperature (20-) 22-28°C.

This species has a large distribution range, and shows a certain amount of variation. A narrow-leaved form from Thailand has been called *A. stachysporus*. It is remarkable in having both flowers and plantlets on the same stem.

Aponogeton lakhonensis
Indo-China. Rhizome 2-4 cm long and 0·5-1·0 cm across. Leaves 20-30 cm long and 1-2 cm broad. Inflorescence unbranched, flowers yellow. A recently imported species which should be cultivated like No. 87.

Aponogeton boivinianus **88**
Northern Madagascar. Rhizome lens-shaped, up to 5 cm across. Leaves 20-60 cm long, 2-5 cm broad, bottle-green, and appearing as though beaten by a hammer. Inflorescence with two or even three spikes, which are bent outwards, the stalks being somewhat thickened above. Growing in fast-flowing rivers. In the aquarium this species can become very large, and it requires good light and a rich substrate. Temperature (16-) 20-24°C. It does not have a well-defined resting period and the leaves are often retained, but the

temperature should be lowered or the rhizome can be taken up and the leaves cut off.

Aponogeton madagascariensis **89**
Madagascar Lace Plant
Madagascar. Rhizome long, up to 3 cm across. Leaf blade up to 20-30 cm long and 8 cm broad. The leaf nerves form a network and the intervening leaf tissue is lacking. There are several forms with differently shaped leaves. Inflorescence with 2-4 (-6) spikes. Growing in fairly fast-flowing waters, both acid and alkaline. This is a curious plant which has fascinated aquarists for a good half century. In the aquarium it is rarely kept for more than a few months, and seldom produces more than 5-10 leaves. It requires bright light, a summer temperature of 18-20°C at the most and a winter temperature of 15-18°C. The water should be changed quite frequently and the substrate should be enriched. Synonyms *A. fenestralis*, *A. henckelianus* and *A. guillotii*.

Najadaceae

Najas guadalupensis **90**
America. Stem erect, branched and easily broken, often sending long roots down into the substrate. Leaves opposite, the edges toothed. Flowers small, in the leaf axils. Growing in lakes and canals. This plant can be easily propagated by cuttings, which quickly take root.

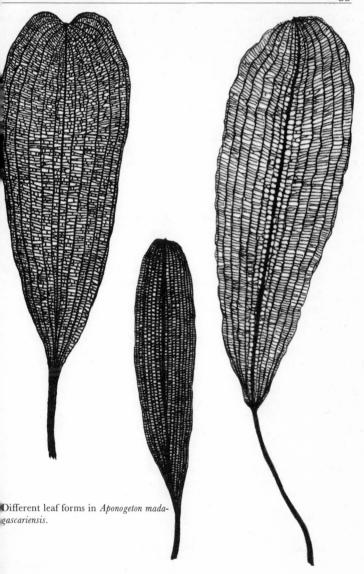

Different leaf forms in *Aponogeton mada-gascariensis.*

It may grow very luxuriantly. Temperature (18-) 20-25°C. Synonym *N. microdon*.

Eriocaulaceae

ERIOCAULON

A large tropical genus of aquatic and marsh plants. Not many species have yet been cultivated in the aquarium.

Eriocaulon sexangulare **91**
Asia. Leaves linear, in rosettes. A weed in paddy fields. In the aquarium it appears that this species requires bright light and some nutrient in the substrate. Temperature 22-28°C.

Xyridaceae

XYRIS

A large tropical genus of predominantly aquatic and marsh plants. Little attention has so far been paid to this genus, but it is likely that several species may be suitable for the aquarium.

Xyris pauciflora **92**
South-east Asia and Australia. Leaves linear, in basal rosettes. Flowers yellow, in a brown head, opening singly. A weed in paddy fields. Temperature 22-28°C. In general, this and the preceding species require the same conditions as No. 64.

Amaryllidaceae

CRINUM

A tropical genus containing a few

aquatic plants. Leaves linear, growing from a bulb. Flowers with 3 pink or white petals, 3 sepals and 6 stamens.

Crinum thaianum **93**
Southern Thailand. Bulb large. Leaves 50-200 cm long, 1-2 (-3) cm broad, linear, without a distinct midrib. Flowers (93c) 10-15 cm in diameter, stamens violet. Seeds 2-3 cm, olive-brown, irregular. Growing in very fast-flowing rivers, often in company with *Barclaya longifolia*, *Cryptocoryne siamensis* and *C. costata*. An undemanding plant which will, however, only attain full size when grown in bright light in a rich substrate. This species is often sold as a seed which has produced a small bulb (93a). Large bulbs (93b) without leaves can with advantage be planted in marshy conditions, when they will rapidly take root. Temperature 22-26°C.

Crinum natans **94**
Central West Africa. Leaves 30-100 cm long, 1-3 cm broad, linear, dark green with a distinct midrib, usually looking as though beaten by a hammer. There are also varieties with leaves that are almost smooth. Seeds about 1 cm long, angular, dark olive-brown. Growing in rivers, often together with *Bolbitis heudelotii* and *Anubias nana*. In the aquarium this species usually thrives in good light and a rich substrate, but it may not produce roots if the bulb has been damaged.

Pontederiaceae

A tropical family of aquatic plants with 8 genera. The growth form and flowers vary according to the genus. Flowers bisexual, often blue, usually with 6 perianth lobes and 3 or 6 stamens, which may vary in length.

Eichhornia crassipes **95**
Water Hyacinth

South America, and introduced in many other parts of the tropics. The floating plants, 10-30 cm tall, have characteristic swollen, air-filled leaf stalks which serve as floats. Rooted plants may reach a height of almost 100 cm. The leaves and leaf stalks vary in form according to the growing conditions. The species is propagated vegetatively by runners which arise in the leaf axils. Flowers pale blue with 6 perianth lobes and 6 stamens. Growing in all types of water where the current is not too fast, sometimes forming very large, coherent populations completely covering the surface and often impeding the passage of boats. This is a very difficult plant to keep in the aquarium, where there must, of course, be plenty of space between the water surface and the glass cover. It requires bright light and some nutrient, including iron, in the absence of which the leaves become yellow. Temperature (18-) 22-28°C.

Eichhornia azurea

Tropical America. Floating plants have rounded leaves, submerse plants have linear leaves arranged in two rows along the stem. Flowers dark blue. This appears to be a difficult plant to cultivate in the aquarium.

Heteranthera zosterifolia **96**

Tropical America. Stem more or less erect, leaves spreading, 3-8 cm long, 3-6 mm broad, linear and flat. Leaves that reach the surface will float. Flowers usually two together, blue, with three stamens, one larger than the other two. Growing in lakes and slow-flowing rivers. A very suitable plant for the aquarium where it requires plenty of light and nutrient. When the stems become too long they can be pruned and the prunings inserted as cuttings. Temperature (18-) 22-26°C.

Zosterella dubia **97**

North and Central America. Similar to the preceding species, but the leaves are twice as long and the internodes longer. Flowers yellow. Growing in lakes and slow-flowing rivers, often in water with a content of calcium. This species grows rapidly and is not suitable for small aquarium tanks. Temperature (15-) 18-22°C. Synonyms *Heteranthera graminea* and *H. dubia*.

Eichhornia azurea.

Araceae

A mainly tropical family of perennial herbaceous plants of which a few genera contain aquatic or marsh plants. The flowers are small and grouped together on an inflorescence known as a spadix which is surrounded by a spathe which is sometimes coloured. The flowers may be bisexual (*Acorus*), slightly reduced and unisexual (*Anubias*) or much reduced and unisexual (*Cryptocoryne*). The spathe may be leaf-like (*Acorus*) and coloured (*Spathiphyllum*) or developed into a specialized tube which encloses the flowers themselves as in *Cryptocoryne*. The leaves grow up more or less directly from the rhizome. The family contains genera with plants containing ethereal oils, bitter substances or cyanogenic compounds. In some genera the leaf cells contain raphides, i.e. groups of small, needle-shaped crystals of calcium oxalate. These raphides and the other compounds are probably the reason fishes do not readily eat the leaves of e.g. *Cryptocoryne*.

Acorus gramineus var. *gramineus* **98**
Eastern Asia. The leaves are a uniform green and 20–30 cm long. The inflorescence consists of a spadix with small flowers, but there is no true spathe. The rhizome is horizontal and branching. The plants grow along the edges of rivers and lakes with the roots in the water. The optimum temperature is 18–20°C, and modern aquaria are a little too warm for this plant. Nevertheless it can live for a long time in such conditions provided the plant is strong and has good roots.

Acorus gramineus var. *gramineus* fol. *variegatis* **99**
A little larger than the preceding form but the leaves have white stripes. Not so suitable for growing underwater.

Acorus gramineus var. *pusillus* **100**
Up to 10 cm tall and with a very tight growth form. More suitable than the two preceding forms for growing underwater, and it will live for years if undisturbed.

ANUBIAS

A small genus of 10–15 species, distributed in West Africa. They have a horizontal, creeping rhizome. The white male flowers consist of 5–6 stamens which lie above the greenish female flowers. The spathe is greenish-white, differing in form according to the species. The species mostly grow in or near rivers.

Anubias nana **101**
Cameroun. 10 (-20) cm tall with round or cordate or ovate leaves. The horizontal rhizome may be very long, with numerous side branches. Living in rivers where the roots form a network which anchors the plants to rocks. *Bolbitis heudelotii*, *Crinum natans* and *Nym-*

phaea zenkeri are often found in similar locations. This species is a good aquarium plant. When grown underwater it is usually not more than 10 cm tall, but treated as a marsh plant it grows taller and flowers quite readily. It should be planted with the rhizome just

Inflorescence of *Anubias nana*.

buried in the surface layer of the substrate, which should contain some nutrient. Temperature 22–26°C.

For some years there has been confusion regarding the name of this plant and it is possibly a dwarf form of *A. barteri*.

Now and again other *Anubias* species appear on the market. They mostly grow more slowly and have poorer root systems.

Anubias afzellii

The leaves are lanceolate and up to 25 cm long. This species grows very well underwater.

Anubias barteri

May grow up to 40 cm tall with the leaf bases broadly ovate or sagittate. When grown underwater it is usually only 15–20 cm tall and the leaves are more rounded. Inflorescence as in *A. nana*.

Anubias congensis

15–25 cm tall. The leaf base is broadly rounded or cordate. The spathe only opens at the tip.

AMAURIELLA

In this genus the anthers are at the top of the male flowers, whereas in *Anubias* they are alongside.

Amauriella auriculata

Up to 50 cm tall with the leaf blade 25 cm. The leaf is broad lanceolate with an auriculate base.

Amauriella hastifolia

About the same size as the preceding species but with hastate leaves.

Male flowers of *Amauriella* (left) and *Anubias* (×4).

Leaf shapes in *Anubias* and *Amauriella*:

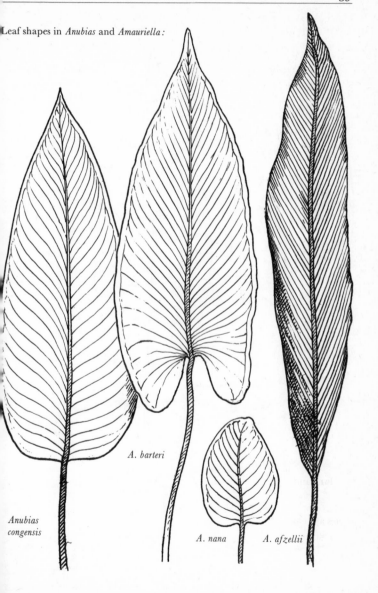

A. barteri

Anubias congensis

A. nana   *A. afzellii*

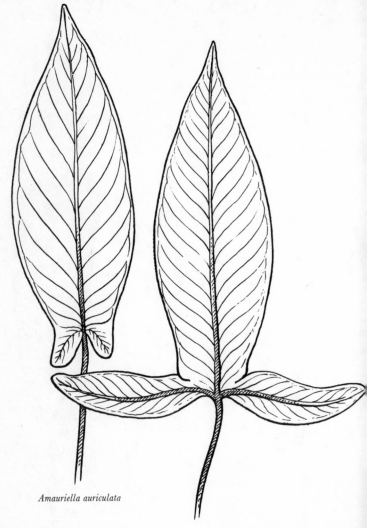

Amauriella auriculata

A. hastifolia

Spathiphyllum wallisii **102**

Northern South America. A very characteristic plant with broad lanceolate, shiny leaves with conspicuous veins. The flowers are bisexual and surrounded by a whitish spathe. In the wild these plants grow in damp places on the forest floor close to rivers. The present species is the most suitable one for the aquarium, and although it is not a true aquarium plant it will grow well when the conditions are favourable. The underwater leaves are narrower and the veins less conspicuous. Temperature 22-25°C. Some strains of this species have sterile flowers and do not set seed. The species can also be grown as a house plant.

Lagenandra thwaitesii.

LAGENANDRA

A genus of marsh plants from India and Sri Lanka. They are closely related to *Cryptocoryne* but differ in that the tubular part of the spathe is shorter and stouter, and the numerous female flowers are arranged spirally and not in a whorl. They are generally coarser plants than *Cryptocoryne* and they mainly grow emerse. The inflorescence lasts some days longer than in *Cryptocoryne*.

Lagenandra ovata **103**

Sri Lanka. A coarse, stiff plant about 100 cm tall with a horizontal rhizome up to 5 cm thick. The leaves are green, lanceolate and smooth. The inflorescence is brownish (red inside) and appears among the numerous basal leaves. This species forms large populations along the rivers in central and south-western Sri Lanka. Even when the waters are high some of the leaves are up above the surface. The species is best grown as a marsh plant when it will reach full size and sometimes flower. When grown underwater it may last for a long time and it makes an outstanding feature in a large tank. Temperature 23-25 (-27)°C.

Lagenandra toxicaria

South India. Distinguished from the preceding species by its lower growth and broader leaves and by having a smooth spathe.

Lagenandra thwaitesii

Sri Lanka. A plant 20-30 cm tall with narrow, slightly rough lanceolate leaves which have a shiny silvery edge (not always apparent). This is a marsh plant which grows well if the light is not too bright. When cultivated underwater there may be difficulty in getting it to take root.

Other species, such as *L. lancifolia* and *L. koenigii*, sometimes appear on the market.

CRYPTOCORYNE

Tropical Asia. A genus with about 50 species in the area from India to the Philippines and New Guinea. They are marsh or water plants with a creeping rootstock and runners. The aerial leaves are often very different from the submerged. The general appearance of the leaves also varies according to the light, water and nutritional factors. This means that the species are often difficult to distinguish from one another. In many cases the only reliable identification character is the form of the inflorescence and spathe. The plants will normally only flower if grown emerse or in shallow water.

In *Cryptocoryne* the spathe is modified to form a tube. At the bottom of the tube there is a whorl of 6-8 female flowers and just above them there are olfactory bodies which produce scent. The very thin spadix rises up from the middle of the whorl of female flowers, carrying at its top some 40 male flowers, each of which consists of two stamens only. Just above the male flowers there is an outgrowth from the spathe which serves to restrict the opening of the tube. The tube starts to widen out at the throat and the upper part is usually petal-like.

When the upper part of the spathe opens, the olfactory bodies start to give off a scent, usually of dung, which attracts insects such as small flies. These land on the upper part of the spathe and crawl or fall down the tube to the female flowers which they pollinate with pollen from other plants which they have brought with them. The insects remain for quite a time down in the base of the inflorescence and about 12 hours after it opened the upper part of the spathe closes again thus trapping the insects. The inflorescence then passes into its male phase, during which the female flowers are no longer receptive to pollen. The insects crawl round in the base of the inflorescence and come in contact with the male flowers, from which they pick up pollen. After about 24 hours the spathe opens again and the insects are free to leave and visit another plant with their new load of pollen. After the third day the spathe withers, but the oval fruit is not ripe until about 3-4 years later. The seeds (2-10 mm long, 1-2 mm wide) are enclosed in a water-repellent waxy coat. They float for a time

and then start to germinate. The seeds die if they become desiccated.

In the aquarium seed formation is not important as the plants produce numerous runners when conditions are favourable. Pieces of rhizome which float at the surface will also produce new plants, which should be planted at a depth of 1-2 cm below the surface of the substrate.

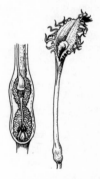

Cryptocoryne ciliata: (right) an inflorescence, (left) the lower end of the spathe removed to show the flowers (enlarged).

It is often said that *Cryptocoryne* looks best when planted in a group. This is quite true but it does not mean that a bunch of 3-5 plants can be just pushed into the substrate. They should, in fact, be planted at a distance of 3-7 cm from one another, depending upon the species. If this is not done they will take a long time to root, and may eventually decay.

During recent years, knowledge

of the genus *Cryptocoryne* has increased considerably. Many of the problems are still unsolved and there are fields in which our knowledge is still insufficient. The relationships of the different species is now better understood, largely on the basis of the chromosome numbers. It has been found that the chromosome numbers can be collected into groups, and that the groups are correlated with the morphology and distribution.

Some 30 species have so far been investigated and the findings can be summarized as follows:

$2n = 22$ or 33 *C. ciliata*, widely distributed in Asia.

$2n = 66, 88$ *C. spiralis*, South India.

$2n = 28, 42$ *C. beckettii* group, Sri Lanka, namely *C. parva* (28), *C. willisii* (28), *C. lucens* (28), *C. beckettii-petchii* (28, 42) and the same for *C. wendtii*, *C. undulata*, *C. lutea-legroi* and *C. walkeri*.

$2n = 30$ *C. pontederiifolia*, Sumatra.

$2n = 34, 68, 102$, is the *C. griffithii* group with *C. griffithii* (34), *C. minima* (34), *C. zewaldiae* (34), *C. affinis* (34), *C. purpurea* (34), *C. siamensis* (68), and *C. blassii* (102), all from Malaya, *C. usteriana* (34) from the Philippines, *C. versteegii* (34), New Guinea, and *C. sarawacensis* (34), Borneo.

$2n = 36, 54, 72$, is the *C. albida* group, India to Indo-China, and the *C. thwaitesii* group. The *C. albida* group has *C. albida* (36), *C. costata* (36), *C. balansae* (36), *C. crispatula* (36, 54) and *C. retrospiralis* (72). The *C. thwaitesii* group has *C. thwaitesii*, *C. alba* and *C. bogneri*, all (36) from Sri Lanka and *C. lingua* (36) from Borneo.

Within the groups the figures show that in many places the species form a polyploidal series, that is plants with multiples of the basic or haploid number of chromosomes. Polyploidy occurs frequently in the plant kingdom and it is an important factor in evolution. In *Cryptocoryne* the numbers explain a number of systematic problems, as for instance in *C. ciliata*, *C. beckettii-petchii* and *C. wendtii* where there are triploid plants as well as diploids. Triploid plants with three times the haploid number of chromosomes are fully viable but they are sterile and so do not set seed. In *Cryptocoryne* the triploids reproduce vegetatively. Similarly, any mutation that occurs will be preserved by vegetative reproduction. *C. wendtii* is a variable species, and of the many forms: brown, green, red and so on, some are triploids with 42 chromosomes, others diploids with 28 chromosomes. The species therefore consists of a number of forms which are more or less genetically constant. *C. petchii* with 42 chromosomes is without doubt to be considered as a triploid of *C. beckettii* ($2n = 28$), and in the same

Cryptocoryne ciliata: runners from (left) a plant with 33 chromosomes and (right) from one with 22 chromosomes.

way there is a diploid and a triploid form of *C. ciliata*. On the other hand, *C. blassii* with 102 chromosomes is probably to be regarded as a sterile hexaploid (6 times the basic number) and *C. siamensis* with 68 as a tetraploid form of a still unknown, yellow-flowered plant with $2n = 34$.

Almost all the species of *Cryptocoryne* have a limited range of distribution. The seeds are large and do not survive desiccation so there are very few chances of dispersal to other river systems, and it is therefore possible that the plants can each evolve in their own way. This is a situation comparable to that found in island groups where evolution has produced a number of closely related but quite distinct species.

In the wild, *Cryptocoryne* grows in or along large and small rivers with more or less direct sunlight. During the monsoon period most species

will be submerged. In the dry season, when the species flower, some will be emerse and others will be in shallow water. In most places the pH is usually about 6 and the water hardness 0-5° DH (German hardness scale). The soil in such places is usually sand and gravel with little calcium, but with variable amounts of mud and plant debris.

In the aquarium the substrate should not be too coarse. Quartz or granite gravel (0·5-5·0 mm) is suitable. The lowermost part of the substrate can with advantage be mixed with some nutrient or even ordinary loam containing some clay.

Some species require plenty of light while others will only live in subdued light.

With air transport from the East large numbers of plants are imported directly from the wild. These plants have had a hard journey, going from the collector to the exporter and then by air to the importer and retail dealer before they reach the aquarist. It is advisable to allow such plants to float at the surface for some days, in subdued light, before they are planted. The substrate in which they are to be planted should not be too old, and a little of the water should be changed. A good water circulation is an advantage, and the light should be subdued for some time after planting. It must, however, be realized that many of these imported plants die as a result of bad handling, but also because some are not really suitable for the aquarium.

Cryptocoryne plants suffer from a condition in which parts of the leaves become glassy and disintegrate. The condition soon spreads and in the course of a day or two a well-planted aquarium can be completely ruined. There is no doubt that this condition is due to the accumulation of waste matter in the water and that things go wrong when this exceeds a certain threshold. The best way to deal with this situation is to change as much of the water as possible and then to clean the tank at the earliest opportunity.

Cryptocoryne ciliata **104**

Tropical Asia. A plant about 100 cm tall with large green leaves. It is characteristic that the spathe has thread-like outgrowths. This plant is found in muddy places near estuaries, often in tidal areas subject to sea water, and usually in full sun. In the aquarium it may grow to a height of 40-50 cm. It requires good light, a temperature of at least 22°C and some nutrient in the substrate.

There are both diploid and triploid forms of this plant. The diploid form with $2n = 22$ has relatively narrow leaves and long (50 cm) runners. The triploid with 33 chromosomes has broader leaves and short, easily breakable runners. There is no difference in spathe form between the two forms. The diploid can set seed while the triploid has sterile flowers.

The vegetative parts somewhat resemble *Lagenandra ovata* (No. 103).

Cryptocoryne spiralis **105**

Southern India. Leaves narrow and up to 50 cm long. The spathe is characterized by the short tube and the long, somewhat twisted upper part which has tooth-like marginal outgrowths. In the aquarium this plant grows slowly, not exceeding 20 cm in height and the leaves often have a brownish tinge. It can tolerate quite low temperatures but prefers 20-26°C, and it requires bright light.

This is a variable species in which two chromosome numbers have so far been found, namely 66 and 88. These are probably hexaploids and octoploids respectively (6 and 8 times the haploid number).

...yptocoryne parva **106**

...i Lanka. A green plant 5-15 cm ...ll with long runners. The leaf ...ade is narrow ovate or almost ...sent. The spathe is not more than ...cm tall. Growing along more or ...ss fast-flowing rivers, often in large ...umbers. In shallow water it grows ...nerse. It prefers places with stable ...il, often among tree roots, and ...ay occur with *C. beckettii* and *C.* ...*tea*. In form and coloration it re- ...mbles a small form of *C. willisii*. ...u the aquarium this species is par- ...cularly suitable for the foreground ...ud it does not usually grow to a ...eight of more than 5 (-10) cm. It ...ows very slowly until well estab- ...hed. Temperature 20-26°C.

...yptocoryne willisii Reitz **107**

...i Lanka. Leaves up to 25 cm long, ...metimes slightly reddish-brown ...u the stalk. The spathe is violet, ...th a yellowish to dark purple ...roat. Growing usually in more ...eltered places than No. 106. One ...'the best species for the aquarium, ...here it does not usually exceed a ...eight of 10 (-15) cm. Once estab- ...hed it sends out numerous run- ...rs. Temperature 20-26°C.

...This species has been cultivated ...an aquarium plant since the turn ...the century, first under the name ...'*beckettii*' and later as *C.* '*nevillii*', ...th erroneous. Without going into ...l the misunderstandings that have ...curred the following is a short ...mmary of the position. In 1908 ...Reitz described some newly im-

ported species of *Cryptocoryne*, including *C. willisii* Reitz and also *C. beckettii*, but the article was subsequently overlooked. In 1909 H. Baum described the same plants, but transposed the names. Baum's *C. willisii* Engl. ex Baum was remembered, and the other species he described later acquired the name *C. nevillii*. In 1955 A. Wendt described a new species, *C. undulata*. This article is, however, not very clear, and among other things he cites *C. willisii* Engler ex Baum as a synonym. Recent investigations (Jacobsen, 1976) have shown that *C. nevillii* Trim. ex Hook. f. is a species which has only been found on two occasions on the east coast of Sri Lanka and has never been in cultivation in Europe. Our 'cultivated nevillii' must therefore have another name and the oldest, valid one is *C. willisii* Reitz. It follows that the name *C. willisii* Engl. ex Baum is nomenclatorily invalid, and that the name to be used for this plant is *C. undulata*. Rataj (1975) used a new name: *C. axelrodii* Rataj, which thus becomes a synonym of *C. undulata*. The fact that around the year 1906 two new, undescribed species were brought to Europe and unintentionally described respectively as *C. willisii* Reitz and *C. willisii* Engl. ex Baum has in the course of time caused considerable trouble. It is interesting that it has in fact taken 70 years to unravel the confusion!

Cryptocoryne beckettii **108**

Sri Lanka. Up to 25 cm tall. Leaf blade bronze-brown to greenish on the upperside, greenish or reddish-violet on the underside. The upper part of the spathe is yellow or brownish, and the throat area brownish-violet. This is one of the least demanding of the *Cryptocoryne* species and can tolerate quite low temperatures and poor light. In the aquarium it does not usually exceed 15 (-20) cm in height. Temperature 20-26°C.

The plant which has been known for some time as *C. petchii*, with 42 chromosomes, is now to be regarded as a triploid form of *C. beckettii* (2n = 28). The form of *C. petchii* cultivated in the aquarium has smallish leaves with wavy edges. There are various forms of both the diploid and triploid plants and it is not really possible to separate the two species.

It is characteristic of the Sri Lanka species within the *C. beckettii* group (Nos. 106-111) that they grow very well as marsh plants, and will then often become larger than submerged specimens.

Cryptocoryne wendtii **109**

Sri Lanka. A species with numerous forms. The spathe has a character-istic twist which partly conceals the brownish to reddish upper part and the blackish-violet throat area. There is considerable variation in leaf form. No. 109 shows the green nominate form (leaf 10-30 cm), No. 109a is a small-leaved form with areas of green and brown (leaf 10-20 cm), No. 109b a small red-leaved form (leaf 10-15 cm), No 109c a large, somewhat brown-leaved form (leaf 15-25 cm) and No. 109d a large form with reddish dented leaves (leaf 20-35 cm). The submerse leaves often have a tend-ency to become slightly dented, as though beaten by a hammer. In contrast to the others in the group, this species usually grows out in the river bed and the leaves are gener-ally larger and thinner. In the aquarium this species grows very quickly and is undoubtedly the best for aquarium use. Tempera-ture 20-26°C.

As in *C. beckettii*, there are both diploid and triploid forms of *C. wendtii*, but the range of variation is even greater.

Cryptocoryne undulata Wendt **110**

Sri Lanka. Normally up to 20 cm in height, but under good conditions up to 30 cm. Leaves narrow and somewhat wavy along the edges, green to brown, with reddish nerves. It is characteristic of this species that the stem has internodes about 1 cm long (also found in some forms of *C. wendtii*) and the plant produces carrot-like runners which easily break off and form new plants (this also occurs in some forms of *C. wendtii*). The spathe is similar in form to that of *C. wendtii*, but the upper part and the throat are yellow or even slightly brownish

In the aquarium this species requires good light and a rich substrate, otherwise the internodes become too long. Temperature 20-26°C. Synonyms *C. willisii* Engl. ex Baum and *C. axelrodi*.

A triploid form has olive-brown leaves that are broader than in the diploid.

Cryptocoryne lutea   **111**
Sri Lanka. Submerse plants up to 15 cm tall, emerse somewhat larger. Leaves very short, green to slightly violet. The plant has a characteristically rigid form. The upper part of the spathe is pure yellow, sometimes greenish; it may have very fine violet dots on the outside and these may also appear in the tube. This plant usually grows rather slowly in the aquarium. Temperature 20-26°C. The triploid form, with larger, more brownish leaves, has been known as *C. legroi*.

Cryptocoryne walkeri
Closely related to the preceding species, but the leaves are slightly larger and often more violet with a more or less wavy edge. The upper part of the spathe has a very large, but not prominent throat area, whereas in *C. lutea* the throat is small but prominent. There are diploid and triploid forms.

Cryptocoryne pontederiifolia   **112**
Sumatra. Up to 30 cm tall. Characterized by the large green cordate leaves which sometimes have short, irregular violet markings. The spathe is very short, red-brown outside, yellow inside, with a large throat. Growing in the fresher parts of tidal waters. Not difficult to keep in the aquarium if there is plenty of light. Temperature 22-26°C.

A plant recently imported into Europe, where it has been known as *C. sulphurea*, has been shown to be identical with *C. pontederiifolia*. The latter name has also been used for a species from Borneo which is really *C. sarawacensis*.

Cryptocoryne sarawacensis   **113**
Borneo. Leaves 10-15 cm long, leaf blades about 5 cm, ovate, green with irregular violet markings. The spathe is drawn out into a long point and is dark violet inside. Growing in somewhat shady places in slow-flowing rivers. This species may be very difficult to keep in the aquarium for it requires soft water with not too much nutrient. Temperature (20-) 22-26°C. Synonyms *C. pontederiifolia* subspecies *sarawacensis* and *C. 'pontederiifolia'*.

Cryptocoryne johorensis   **114**
Malaya. Leaves pointed cordate, somewhat wavy along the edges, green to brownish-green with violet markings. The spathe has a long white tube and a long pointed upper part. Growing in small forest streams. Not difficult to cultivate, but it may not be easy to be certain of its correct identification. It requires subdued light and slightly

acid water rich in nutrient. Temperature 22-26°C. The plant illustrated is an emerse specimen with small, spreading leaves. Submerse plants have larger, more erect leaves.

Cryptocoryne schulzei **115**
Malaya. Leaves up to 20 cm long, violet-brown with dark markings. The spathe is yellowish with a characteristic recurved tip. Growing in small streams. First described in 1972, this species thrives in the same conditions as No. 116.

Cryptocoryne minima **116**
Malaya. Up to 10-15 cm tall. Leaf blades ovate, 2-4 cm long, dark green on the upperside, pale green with reddish-violet veins on the underside. Spathe 2-3 cm, the upper part usually recurved, dark red with a warty surface. Growing in small shady forest streams. This species requires subdued light and a rich substrate. It is sometimes difficult to keep for any length of time, but once established it reproduces readily. Temperature 22-26°C.

Cryptocoryne griffithii **117**
Malaya. Up to 15-20 cm tall. Leaf blades 5-10 cm long, rounded cordate, dark green on the upperside, reddish-violet on the underside. Spathe 5-10 cm long, red to dark reddish-violet with a warty upper part and a conspicuous throat area. Growing in slow-flow-

ing streams. Aquarium conditions as for No. 116.

This plant was first introduced for aquarium use during the last 5-10 years. The plant formerly cultivated as *C. 'griffithii'* is in fact *C. purpurea*.

Cryptocoryne purpurea **118**
Malaya. Up to 15-30 cm tall. Leaf blades 5-10 cm, pointed and broad ovate, the upperside green, usually with an irregular violet pattern, the underside pale green with pale violet-red veins and often an irregular reddish-violet pattern. Spathe 10-15 cm, the upper part red, the throat area large, pale red to yellowish. Growing in slow-flowing forest streams. This is not a difficult plant to keep in the aquarium, where it does best in a rich substrate and in subdued light. Temperature (20-) 22-26°C. Synonym *C. hejnyi*.

For many years this plant was grown under the erroneous name *C. griffithii*.

Cryptocoryne blassii **119**
Malaya and southern Thailand. Up to 20-40 cm tall. Leaf blades more or less ovate, usually somewhat dented, violet on the upperside and paler on the underside. Spathe 10-15 cm, the upper part yellow, with a large throat. Growing in slow-flowing forest streams. This species should preferably be cultivated in a rich substrate and does best in subdued light. Tem-

perature (20-) 22-26°C.

This plant is a hexaploid with 102 chromosomes, and the flowers are sterile. It can, therefore, be regarded as forming a single population, which reproduces exclusively by vegetative means (see *C. siamensis*).

Cryptocoryne siamensis
Malaya. Similar to the preceding species but differing in having broader, pointed ovate leaves and a spathe with the upper part drawn out to a longer tip; there are also minor differences in the female flowers.

The chromosome number is 68, and the plant is a tetraploid. So far a plant with $2n = 34$ resembling *C. siamensis-blassii* has not been found, and until the whole complex of *C. siamensis*, *C. blassii*, *C. kerri*, *C. cordata*, *C. grandis* and *C. grabowskii* has been investigated in more detail it is not possible to say anything definite about their systematic status.

Cryptocoryne usteriana **120**
Philippines. Up to 1·5 m tall, with large, lanceolate, dented green leaves. The spathe is matt reddish-violet with the upper part irregularly twisted. Often growing submerse in fairly slow-flowing rivers. This is a rewarding plant to grow in the aquarium and with good light and a rich substrate it will soon become quite large. It even thrives in hard water. Runners are

produced very readily. Temperature (20-) 22-26°C. This plant is similar to *C. balansae* but can be distinguished by the prominent lateral ribs which arise a little above the leaf base. Synonym *C. aponogetonifolia*.

Cryptocoryne affinis **121**
Malaya. Leaves up to 50 cm long, dented or smooth, green or reddish on the upperside, violet on the underside. Spathe with the upper part much twisted and blackish-violet. Growing in slow-flowing, shady forest streams. This species does well in the aquarium and adapts to a variety of conditions, but only reaches its full size when planted in a rich substrate. Temperature (18-) 22-26°C. Synonym *C. haerteliana*.

Cryptocoryne versteegii **122**
New Guinea. Up to 10-15 cm tall, with rounded triangular, fleshy, green leaves. Spathe with a short red upper part and a prominent yellow throat. Growing in muddy places in the lower reaches of the rivers. This species requires good light and a rich substrate, but even so it grows very slowly. Temperature (20-) 22-26°C.

Cryptocoryne lingua **123**
Borneo. Up to 10-20 cm tall, with spatulate, fleshy, green leaves. Spathe with the upper part much elongated. Growing in muddy places in the lower reaches of rivers.

In the aquarium it requires good light and a rich substrate, but is often difficult to keep for any length of time. Temperature 22-26°C.

Cryptocoryne thwaitesii **124**
Sri Lanka. Leaves 10-15 cm long, the leaf blades ovate, green to violet, the upperside matt, the edges somewhat toothed. Submerse leaves become narrower and more violet. Spathe white, with red dots inside, and drawn out to a long point which often turns forwards. Growing in small, shady forest streams, often emerse. In the aquarium this species should be grown in slightly acid water with a rich substrate and subdued light. It grows slowly and is rather difficult to keep. Temperature 22-26°C.

Cryptocoryne balansae **125**
Indo-China. Leaves linear to lanceolate, 30-60 cm long, 2-4 cm broad, usually dented, green or brownish. Emerse plants are often somewhat smaller. The spathe is more or less spirally twisted, and has short or long violet markings. There is no distinct throat area. Growing in or along the banks of rivers, even where the water has a content of calcium. This species is sometimes difficult to keep in the aquarium. It requires good light and a rich substrate. Temperature (20-) 22-26°C.

Several different forms have been imported during recent years. These include one with smooth,

brownish leaves 10-20 cm long and 0·5-1 cm broad, and another with brown or green leaves 20-30 cm long and only 0·5 cm broad. These are very similar to *C. crispatula* and if future investigations show that they are all one species then the correct name will be *C. crispatula*.

Cryptocoryne costata **126**
Southern Thailand. Leaves lanceolate, up to 30 cm, brownish with irregular violet stripes. Spathe with a short, twisted upper part with a recurved tip and red dots on the inside. Growing in and along the banks of rivers, often in full sun. In the aquarium it must therefore have good light, but is otherwise not difficult to keep, although it grows rather slowly.

Cryptocoryne albida
Burma and southern Thailand. Similar to the preceding species, but the leaves are green. The spathe has a longer, twisted upper part and long, red-brown markings. It is possible that this plant and *C. costata* are actually one and the same species, in which case the valid name would be *C. albida*. Synonyms *C. hansenii*, *C. korthausae*, and *C. retrospiralis* subspecies *albida*.

Cryptocoryne retrospiralis **127**
India, Bangladesh and Burma. Leaves lanceolate to linear, up to 50 cm long, green, often slightly brownish at the base. The winter leaves are more or less cylindrical.

The plant has long runners with numerous roots. Spathe somewhat twisted and yellowish with large reddish markings. Growing in sandy places in rivers, often in shallow water and with emerse leaves. This species is often difficult to keep in the aquarium. It requires bright light and a rich substrate. Temperature (18-) 22–26°C.

This species has been misinterpreted for some years. Recent reports have often referred to plants of the *C. crispatula* type. It first arrived in Europe in 1972 and is therefore not widely distributed as an aquarium plant.

Pistia stratiotes **128**
Water Lettuce
Cosmotropical. A floating plant with ovate, bluish-green, hairy leaves in rosettes. The inflorescence, arising from a leaf axil, consists of one female flower and several male flowers within a whitish spathe about 1 cm long. Vegetative reproduction is by runners. This is a common weed in lakes and slow-flowing rivers throughout the tropics, often completely covering the surface. It can multiply so fast that the outermost plants are pushed up on to the banks. It requires bright light and water rich in nutrient. In the aquarium it does not usually grow very large and it acquires a characteristic flattish growth form, with the leaves lying out over the water surface. Temperature 22–28°C. It is advisable to keep it over the winter in a tank with earth and peat at a temperature of 18–20°C.

Lemnaceae

A cosmopolitan family of floating plants, which consist of a very short stem and a leaf-like thallus. Roots may be several, one or absent. Flowers without a perianth, unisexual. The male flower consists of one stamen, the female of one ovule. Vegetative reproduction is by budding off new thalli.

Lemna minor **129**
Lesser Duckweed
Cosmopolitan. Floating, oval, flat thalli, 2–3 mm in diameter, with one root to each thallus, the root tip rounded. Budding takes place from a small pouch at the edge of the thallus. Inflorescence with one female and two male flowers. This

Lemna minor and root tips of *L. paucicostata* and *L. minor*.

tiny plant usually thrives in the aquarium, and may cover the water surface completely, thus preventing light from reaching the other plants.

Lemna paucicostata
Tropics and subtropics. Similar to the preceding species, but differing in having pointed root tips. Often introduced with other aquatic plants from Asia.

Lemna trisulca **130**
Ivy-leaved Duckweed
Very widely distributed, except in South America. Submerse, bottle-green, translucent, cruciform plants, with thalli 1·2 cm long. When in flower the plants float up to the surface. Common in slightly acid lakes. Temperature 16-22°C.

Spirodela polyrhiza **131**
Greater Duckweed
Cosmopolitan, but not found in Africa. Leaves floating, dark green with a slight violet tinge on the upper surface, violet or reddish on the under surface, circular, 5-8 mm in diameter, with several roots from each thallus segment. In lakes, ponds and canals. An easy plant to keep in the aquarium, but the violet colour only appears in bright light. Synonym *Lemna polyrhiza*.

Wolffia arrhiza **132**
Rootless Duckweed
Widely distributed except in colder areas. Plants floating free at the surface, singly or two together,

ellipsoid, slightly flat on the upperside, 0·5-1·5 mm long. Roots absent. Inflorescence with only one male and one female flower in a depression on the upperside. Growing in lakes and ponds. This species requires good light and sufficient nutrient, but is not easy to keep in the aquarium.

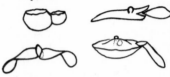

Enlarged drawings of (top, left to right) *Wolffia*, *Wolffiopsis* and (bottom, left to right) *Wolffiella*, *Pseudowolffia*.

Wolffia microscopia
South-east Asia. Similar to the preceding species but even smaller, about 0·5 mm. One of the world's smallest flowering plants.

Wolffiella lingulata
Western North America and Mexico. Thallus flat, often curved, with one male and one female flower on the upperside.

Wolffiopsis welwitschii
Tropical Africa and America. Thallus flat, ovate and slightly curved. Two tiny inflorescences on the upperside, each with one male and one female flower.

Pseudowolffia hyalina
Africa. Thallus lens-shaped, with one male and one female flower on the upperside.

Cyperaceae

A large family with 70 genera and about 3,500 species, mostly growing in wet or damp places. Only a few species are cultivated in the aquarium.

Eleocharis acicularis **133**
Needlegrass, Hairgrass
Cosmopolitan. Rhizome creeping, sending up stems 5-15 cm long from the internodes. Leaves small, membranous, arising from the base of the stems which they enclose in a sheath. Flowers bisexual, usually 6-8 in a spikelet. Growing along the edges of lakes and forming extensive carpets. In the aquarium this species should be planted in sand or fine gravel with a little soil, and given plenty of light. Temperature (15-) 20-25°C.

Eleocharis vivipara
South-eastern North America. Larger than the preceding species, 10-30 cm tall, and forming new plants from the flower axils. This species is rather difficult to keep in the aquarium. Temperature (18-) 20-24°C.

Eleocharis vivipara.

Poaceae

A very large family of grasses with 700 genera and about 8,000 species, of which a few grow in marshy places.

Hygrorhyza aristata **134**
South-east Asia. Floating at the surface with the help of the inflated leaf sheaths. Leaves often with one or more brown markings. Roots finely divided. Inflorescences in the form of a panicle with a few flowers, each with a long pedicel or stalk. A weed in paddy fields, this plant may be difficult to keep in an aquarium tank if there is insufficient space between the water surface and the glass cover. It requires bright light and water rich in nutrient. The plant reaches its maximum size when rooted in the substrate. Temperature (18-) 22-28°C.

Bibliography

Cook, C. D. K. (1974) *Water plants of the world* W. Junk, The Hague.

Fasset, N. (1955) 'Echinodorus in the American tropics' *Rhodora* **57,** 133–156, 174–188, 202–212.

Jacobsen, N. (1976) 'Notes on the Cryptocoryne of Sri Lanka' *Botaniska Notiser* **129,** 179–190.

Jacobsen, N. (1977) 'Chromosome numbers and taxonomy in Cryptocoryne' *Botaniska Notiser* **130,** 71–87.

Sculthorpe, C. D. (1967) *The biology of aquatic vascular plants* Edward Arnold, London.

The following periodicals will also be of interest.

Freshwater and Marine Aquarium, R/C Modeler Corporation Inc., Sierra Madre, California, U.S.A.

Pet Fish: Practical Fishkeeping Monthly, PF Publications, London.

Tropical Fish Hobbyist, TFH Publications Inc., Neptune City, New Jersey, U.S.A. and Reigate, England.

Index of Latin Names

Numbers in **bold** type are plate numbers; the descriptions of the plants are arranged in order of plate number on pages 97-155. Where there is no plate the page number of the description is given. Page numbers in *italics* refer to line drawings of plants when these illustrations appear on a different page from their descriptions.

Index of English Names